*Stardogs*

Critical acclaim for *Stardogs* and *Starcats*:

# Stardogs

## astrology for dogs

## (and owners)

**HELEN HOPE**

Ulysses Press

Published by Ulysses Press
      P.O. Box 3440
      Berkeley CA 94703
      www.ulyssespress.com

Library of Congress Control Number 2002101473
ISBN 1-56975-308-3

First published in Australia in 2002 by HarperCollins*Publishers* Pty Limited

Printed in Canada by Transcontinental Printing

10 9 8 7 6 5 4 3 2 1

Cover and internal illustrations by Karen Young
Cover design and internal design by Melanie Feddersen, i2idesign

# CONTENTS

# INTRODUCTION

The dog, Canis familiaris, is a noble creature that, from time immemorial, has linked its fortunes to humankind and helped us in our struggle through to the present era. Without the help of the dog, would we have been so successful in early hunting days; without the protection of the dog, would as many of us have survived in a world bristling with hungry and much stronger predators, many of them afoot at night when we need sleep?

We humans have many reasons to thank our four-footed friend the dog. Not only has it pulled our sleighs, rounded up the sheep, herded the cows, kept watch at night and performed numerous other services, it has also loved us with a steadfast love, and has entertained, amused and educated us. There is no doubt that this canine is a special creature. Just how special was revealed to me in a rather amazing way.

Many years ago, after having lived overseas, we were househunting in earnest, longing to put down roots again. Finally we decided on a lovely old home with bay windows, a pool and a tennis court, a short walk from a secluded bay, and completely surrounded by a large and lush reserve much used by the Boy

Scouts. However, the original family (the father of whom had been a decorated captain of the Light Horse Cavalry in the First World War) was still in possession of the house, and would only sell it provided we took on Sol, their beautiful pedigree collie, who was now rather advanced in years and had never known any other home. And so, of course, we agreed.

It took a little while, but Sol did unfreeze towards us. He especially loved it when my children were splashing around in the pool—he became a pup again, running around barking and playing with the kids, having a marvelous time. Sol tolerated me, but he loved Gawayne and Belindalee. Time marched on and Sol, already very old, began to fail. We tried everything but, as the vet pointed out, it came down to the fact that his body was worn out. As each week went by he became more and more frail. None of us wanted to put him to sleep, but neither did we want Sol to suffer. When it got to where Sol was unable to move and obviously was not going to get any better, with a heavy heart I knew it was time to phone for the vet. He tried to assuage my feelings by assuring me that Sol wouldn't suffer, and he arranged to come to the house on the following day.

With tears blurring my eyes, I got in the car to get groceries from the nearby village. Sol had been put under the macrocarpa hedge to rest in the sun and fresh air. As I was leaving I noticed the door of the fenced tennis court was open. But as Sol was a long way from it and he could hardly move I kept going. Upon my return he was not to be seen! Amazed, I headed straight for the tennis court, sure that he would never have been able to cross it. Total consternation. He wasn't there. But the door on the other side of the court was also open. So we mounted a search—down to the beach, around the grounds and reserve, telephoning the scout headquarters to ask if they might have spotted Sol; they knew him well, but they hadn't seen him. By the time night fell Sol hadn't been found. How an extremely feeble and almost immobilized dog could completely disappear was utterly beyond me. I soothed the children as best I could and finally fell, dead tired, into bed myself. I was thinking of nothing and sinking into a deep sleep when suddenly, as if a window had opened in my mind, there was Sol! He was standing in the shallows of our little beach, looking like a much younger version of himself. All his feathers were flying as he looked intently out to the horizon over the incoming tide. It was the strangest experience. It was a little like Sol was aware of my consciousness but was completely focused, and not to be distracted from his expectant attention on the horizon for what he was waiting with utter certainty. I sat up, shook my head, then lay down and went straight to sleep.

That dream vision took place on Wednesday. The following day we searched again, fully expecting to discover Sol. But Thursday came and went, and the mystery continued. And it was ditto for Friday. But on Saturday around noon we had a phone call from scout headquarters. There had been a huge influx of Boy Scouts for an activities weekend, in the course of which every nook and cranny of the reserve had been penetrated. And a patrol had found Sol. He was deep in the underbrush, up a little hill, with his head next to the tree on top of it. We were all awed and hushed as we stood there. Sol had gone to greet his own death like some almighty warrior, summoning up supernatural energy to do so. And I knew, without any doubt, that it was his spirit leaving the earthly realm that I had been privileged to witness on that Wednesday night.

All members of the dog kingdom are stars, and this book has been written in their honor. I didn't know Sol's date of birth, but my deductions would be that he was a double Leo. His aristocracy and nobility were strongly evident, and his name "Sol" means "sun" in French. The Sun, of course, rules Leo.

I am sure your dog is every bit as magnificent a creature as Sol, so please read on to gain even more insight into your splendid canine comrade's depth of character.

# ATTRIBUTES

If you don't know your dog's date of birth, for whatever reason, read through the following chart to see which star tribe your pet's personality and habitual behavior corresponds with.

**KEY**

SIGN ●
KEY WORDS ○
ATTRIBUTES ●

**ARIES**

courageous;
enthusiastic;
independent;
impulsive; impatient;
headstrong; selfish;
aggressive

fiery,
dynamic character;
high energy; risk-taker;
rebellious; competes for
affection; leaps at postal
workers; enjoys playing with
humans; fights; sense of
superiority; physically
strong

loyal;
trustworthy;
reliable; persevering;
possessive; lazy;
compassionate;
stubborn

affectionate;
peaceful; would
travel miles to find
owner; loves sleep and
comfort; eager to please;
loves routine; loathes
change; melodious voice;
smells flowers

**TAURUS**

**GEMINI**

friendly; versatile; perceptive; restless; contradictory; critical; eloquent; impatient; vocal

super-alert; loves to be talked to; inquisitive; hates to be leashed; busy; fun-loving; enjoys people; not demonstrative; high-strung; good at doing tricks

sympathetic; protective; moody; industrious; sociable; sensitive; argumentative; emotional; psychic

thrives on affection; noble nature; sits at owner's feet; has rich fantasy life; can be silly; nips at rivals; loves to lick; great parent

**CANCER**

regal; optimistic; affectionate; self-centered; indolent; devoted; sunny nature; demanding; domineering; generous; enthusiastic

**LEO**

proud; bestows glorious love on owner; barks a lot; holds grudges; dislikes strangers in home; loves sunset or sunrise walks; good at tricks finicky; considerate; aloof; intelligent; busy; self-absorbed; systematic; reliable; industrious; shy; faithful

**VIRGO**

excels in master–dog relationship; attention to detail; well-groomed; enjoys routine; rarely demonstrative; prefers quiet life; senses if something amiss; soft-hearted; curious; fussy eater

cooperative; sociable; indecisive; lazy; diplomatic; helpful; vocal; dependent; eager

**LIBRA**

popular; stylish; loves being seen with owner; unpredictable; has sweet tooth; prefers leisure and companionship to work; occasionally prone to foolish behavior

**SCORPIO**

brave; resourceful; ambitious; intuitive; obstinate; determined; jealous; vengeful; efficient

"command" presence—rarely has to fight; hard to "read"; forms strong bonds with owner; nurses hurts; non-conformist; protective to children; hardy

fun-loving; makes people laugh; a charming wanderer; loathes being tied down; loves showing off; exuberant; contemplative; can seem human; enjoys music; easily side-tracked

cheerful; versatile; friendly; quarrelsome; boastful; engaging; irresponsible; loud; charismatic

**SAGITTARIUS**

patient; responsible; goal-driven; intolerant; sensible; suspicious; capable; practical; clever; reliable

takes relationship with owner seriously; avoids risk; cool in a crisis; purposeful; great zest for life; fabulous memory; undemanding; needs to feel wanted

**CAPRICORN**

social,
intuitive,
unpredictable,
inventive, rebellious,
intelligent, helpful,
independent, single-
minded

rugged
individualist; life is
a continual experiment;
freedom-loving; not cuddly;
easily bored; cheers up owner;
hearty appetites; befriends all
types of humans and
creatures

**AQUARIUS**

**PISCES**

psychic;
sympathetic;
indecisive; changeable;
hypersensitive;
impressionable;
devoted;
enchanting

dependent
on owner's love; has
big highs and lows;
gentle and intuitive; flees
when stressed; adores the
outdoors; enjoys
watching TV

# ARIES
*dog*

21 March–20 April

**tree:** Hawthorn

**metal:** Iron

**day:** Tuesday

**element:** Fire

**deepest dream:** To be a Viking's dog

**typical Aries dog:** Inspector Rex—Austrian television show

THE ARIES DOG CAN BE **AGGRESSIVE**, BUT MUCH OF THAT IS BLUSTER (EXCEPT FOR WHEN ANOTHER ANIMAL IS SEEN TO BE EXTENDING A LEADERSHIP CHALLENGE). IT LIKES AND NEEDS A LOT OF ACTION WITH **YOU**. IT WANTS TO BE IN ON EVERYTHING THE HOUSEHOLD DOES BECAUSE THIS POOCH DEFINITELY REGARDS ITSELF AS ONE OF THE FAMILY. AND THIS WORTHY ANIMAL GIVES ITS HEART, SOUL AND **DEVOTION** FOREVER. BEING AN ARIES DOG, WHEN IT GIVES ITS TRUST IT DOES SO WITH ETERNAL, **PASSIONATE** CONVICTION.

**T**he Aries dog is ruled by Mars, planet of war or constructive action. You, dear owner, will be looked to as the guiding principle in expressing these drives. Understanding your sometimes willful canine's nature will be of great assistance in this matter.

A keyword for Aries pooches is **passionate**—and they are keyed right into the moment. For example, if someone or something is heard approaching the house they're outside in a flash, letting everyone know that here is a super warlike canine that will fight to the death and **vanquish** all corners. That is if it doesn't take too long, because it can get bored rather quickly (into the moment, remember).

These qualities can get you and your energetic pet into trouble if you take to the streets without having had any dog obedience training. Especially when your Aries dog, whose ego can be about the size of Uluru, feels provoked by what it deems "lesser animals." But if it is given plenty of exercise (like long walks, running on the beach, playing ball), and obedience training, your Mars-inspired dog will become a lot less militant, and much more manageable. This kind of regime also takes care of Aries dogs' propensity (prompted by their enthusiastic loving nature) to leap at the special people in their life, and knock the groceries/packages/person helter skelter.

If there are other animals in the house your Aries hound is likely to become competitive. It simply can't stand it if another animal seems to take first place in your affections and will do all in its power to appear in the best light. If that means nudging the cat out the door when you're not looking (or even if you are in the early stages of this duel), then that's what it'll do.

This red hot creature can be rather excitable, but that's part and parcel of its passionate nature, which is strongly evident in its love of life and love for you. Your Aries dog may zoom off on tangents. A rustle in the grass, an **active**-looking person, an especially good smell wafting past, and it can be gone. (It may be best to use a leash when out walking, especially during puppy days.) However, Aries pooches are never gone for long. Risk takers they may be, but their forays never take them far as they absolutely **hate** to be out of the center of your attention for too long. They always want to share the action with **you**!

Your Aries canine is usually pretty happy, and sure that there is bound to be a positive outcome to life—even when you've had to chastise them for chewing up your new slippers or the new postal worker's pants! They are confident there'll be a good meal at the end of the day, which they normally wolf down, and possibly seconds if they can impress you enough with their charismatic eyes. Another one of their certainties is that after some misdemeanor you will **always** pet them eventually. Others are that you **love** them, and will sometimes romp around with them.

Your Aries pup will probably inadvertently do things that displease you. But after being made aware that a particular behavior is not appropriate, a little prompting from you helps your pet not to repeat it. There's a quick intelligence inside that doggy head. It would never want to hurt you, and most likely won't have a malicious bone in its body. (Except, of course, when dealing with canine upstarts who think they're the local leaders. Your dog sees them as begging for the full fury treatment, and so gives it to them. As they do with any real threat to the household.) The big picture is that your pet genuinely wants to please you, it's just that sometimes its own short-term needs and desires get in the way. But when it has a clear picture of what you want it to do, it can be highly responsible in keeping up that behavior—perhaps not quite so diligently as the dutiful Virgo dog down the road, whom your dog considers boring but does note that they've got their paper routine down. And this reminds your pooch to do its best, so that its superiority can be demonstrated.

The Aries dog rarely grumbles about what its tasks and responsibilities are either because, on the whole, it's generally happy performing its duties. (If ever it isn't, then it conveniently forgets to do them!) It's likely that you often hear people say, "Looks like that dog of yours is smiling" as your Aries woofer lopes about (it hardly ever walks!), fetching the stick or paper, or simply loping about.

**TO SUM UP:** The Aries dog can be aggressive, but much of that is bluster (except for when another animal is seen to be offering a leadership challenge). It likes and needs a lot of action with **you**. It wants to be in on everything the household does because this pooch definitely regards itself as one of the family. And this worthy animal gives its heart, soul and devotion forever. Being an Aries dog, when it gives its trust it does so with eternal, **passionate** conviction.

An Aries dog is super-charged. It is strong, both physically and in terms of spirit. You have a wonderful loyal animal. What would hit it hardest is if it was ever betrayed in any way. Also, if possible, never chain or lock up your dog for long periods. With plenty of exercise and hearty food you will have a great friend, capable of surprising you with unexpected brilliance.

# TAURUS *dog*

21 April–20 May

**tree:** Apple

**metal:** Copper

**day:** Friday

**element:** Earth

**deepest dream:** Secretly wants to be a St. Bernard or a lap dog

**celebrity dog:** Dogmatrix—Asterix's dog of comic-book fame

BEING BASICALLY A STRONG ANIMAL WITH A GOOD CONSTITUTION AND A REASONABLY **PLACID** NATURE (UNLESS THE BOUNDARIES GET CROSSED), THE TAUREAN DOG IS UNLIKELY TO NEED MUCH CODDLING. JUST BE SURE TO SHOW YOUR PET EVERYDAY, EVEN IF IT'S IN A SMALL WAY, THAT YOU LOVE IT, AND IT'LL REMAIN CONTENTED. AND DON'T FORGET IT THRIVES ON ITS WALKS AND ITS FOOD. WITH THESE AREAS TAKEN CARE OF IT'S A DOG IN PARADISE. THEN ITS GREAT LOVE OF LIFE KNOWS **NO BOUNDS**, AND YOU, ITS **ADORED** OWNER, ARE BLESSED WITH ONE CONSTANT IN THIS WORLD OF CHANGE: YOUR PET'S DEEP AND UNDYING LOVE FOR YOU.

**T**he Taurean dog is ruled by Venus, goddess of love and pleasure. Basically, this star hound responds rather enthusiastically to its master's call, because it knows it means the good times are going to roll almost without fail. And this pooch dearly loves a good time—even if it would like to dictate the terms!

Understanding your canine's Taurean nature will deepen the already profound bond between you. You've probably already observed that your Taurean dog's attitude towards life is what might be termed "fixed"—especially when in more senior doggy years. To illustrate: your dog finds it disturbing if you don't arrive home at the usual time, but steadfastly (and forgivingly!) it will continue to wait. You may think that this behavior only stems from thoughts of dinner (although it must be said food is extraordinarily important to your Taurean animal), but really it's because **you** are the pivot of its universe. This fixed quality can also be observed when on an outing together you give the command, "Stay." Your pooch usually does just that, and with a sense of pride—unlike some canine cousins, who find it hard to keep still. For instance, your dog considers the Gemini dog, a "flibberty gibbet," and looks on in scorn as it chases after shadows.

This Taurean nature endows your animal with a great capacity for love, and it gives all its affection to you. (It is one of the most faithful and loyal animals possible. When its mind is made up, there's precious little that can change it!) It will follow wherever you lead. Your tactile creature will also take all the petting, caressing and soft words you can bestow. It is important to your Taurean dog to be made tangibly aware that you love it. (They're not like some Aquarian dogs, who can function merely on eye contact!) The Taurean hound needs lots of love, cuddles, hugs and soothing words. It tends to have a rather fine voice itself, and rather fancies its abilities in that area. When it howls or barks it's usually in well-rounded tones!

Your Taurus woofer will always take notice of you, and if aware of displeasing you in any way will instantly begin to phase out the offending behavior. Yet it may seem to you at times (particularly during puppy days) that your canine is a little slow to catch on! And its tendency towards ebullient clumsiness definitely diminishes after a simple obedience course. But *comme si, comme ça,* all this is just part and parcel of Taurus Dog's placid, loving nature.

There's a tad of "dogmatism" (pun unavoidable) about your pooch, but where you, dear owner, are concerned, only in their love and devotion for you. (The dog who travels thousands of miles to find its owner is a Taurean dog for sure!) And its behavior will always be modified to please you. But in other ways a Taurus pooch's dogma holds sway. If the dog down the street, for example, breaches your four-legged friend's code of what is acceptable, then that's **it**! Never again will their noses touch. And your dog doesn't much care for change. If things must alter, say there's a house move, for instance, then so be it and they'll go along with it. But they **hate** it. They'd much prefer to stay where everything is familiar and known. The Taurean dog is just not that happy about charging off into the unknown.

Taurus canines also tend towards being jealous. So when you make a big fuss of a visiting dog or person, you're likely to find your pooch sulking in a corner somewhere later. On the other hand, your hound can be easily affectionate towards other people (unless, of course, the person triggers its negative "dogmatism" buttons). It's just the way they are. But no one, repeat **no one**, means more to your Taurean dog than you do. You are the most important thing in their world, and they would go through fire to be with you.

Being reasonably gentle animals, as long as little children don't tease or irritate them, Taurus dogs are pretty good with small people. Peace and harmony is important to this pooch. It can become quite upset if people argue, or if bad feelings are rampant. The Aries dog may find that sort of situation stimulating, but definitely not the Taurean. Yet, this doesn't mean your dog is a coward. Far from it. If it decides to take a stand there's not much that can shift it. For example, anyone attempting to break into your house would have to deal with an immovable force, one that will also bark and bite with great tenacity.

Harsh conditions hold little appeal for the Taurean pooch. If it can't occupy your bedroom or pride of place in the living room, then their ideal spot is an air-conditioned, centrally heated, shag-pile-floored, velvet-lined dog abode ("kennel" to the uninitiated), where the food and liquid refreshments arrive nonstop. No doubt about it, your canine **adores** comfort. Lying in the sun is also something they love to do. Some may label that lazy, but that's not the case at all. What they're doing at these times is ruminating upon (to them) **great** and **important** matters. Like their favorite person, you, their upcoming dinner, and/or the nice dog up the street. Having such a rich imaginative life, the Taurean dog doesn't usually make a good cattle dog. (Although people can be forgiven for getting the wrong idea because of the bull's association with this sign. But think about it! A bull's more likely to be reclining in the sun than rounding up the herd.) However, whatever you want, your animal will almost always try to fulfill your wishes because its urge to please you is very strong.

Going walking is a favorite Taurean dog occupation, especially if it's with you. But when that's not possible your pooch is happy to go off wandering. This will be nothing too vigorous or dangerous, just a happy perambulation among interesting smells (the Taurean woofer is known for smelling flowers as well as lampposts) and sights. One of its favorite haunts is the countryside, where it roams the many meadows. But when living in the city the Taurus pooch enjoys the parks just as much. The open air and abundant space where Mother Nature holds sway is where your fine canine is happiest.

**TO SUM UP:** Being basically a strong animal with a good constitution and a reasonably placid nature (unless the boundaries get crossed, as explained earlier), the Taurean dog is unlikely to need much coddling. Just be sure to show your pet everyday, even if it's in a small way, that you love it, and it'll remain contented. And don't forget it thrives on its walks and its food. With these areas taken care of it's a dog in paradise. Then its great love of life knows no bounds, and you, its adored owner, are blessed with one constant in this world of change, your pet's deep and undying love for you.

The Taurean dog is a gem. However, do make sure that negative behavior patterns don't build up, as you'll have a particularly difficult job changing any behavior that your dog has formed after repeated occurrences of "getting away with it." Also be careful about what flea collars or even ordinary collars you choose, as the neck is a highly sensitive area. Weight can also be a problem if your pet's allowed to gorge. But with these matters taken care of, you'll have a loving, peaceful animal in your life that will love you forever.

# GEMINI *dog*

21 May–21 June

**tree:** Jacaranda

**metal:** Quicksilver

**day:** Wednesday

**element:** Air

**deepest dream:** Greatest wish is to move at the speed of light

**celebrity dog:** Gromit—from Wallace and Gromit

ON YOUR PET'S BEHALF, AND WITHOUT ANY FALSE MODESTY, IT CAN BE SAID YOU HAVE AN INTERESTING ANIMAL AND WORTHY COMPANION. THAT TENDENCY TO NOT ALWAYS DO THINGS IN THE SAME WAY AND TO COME UP WITH SOMETHING **DIFFERENT** WHEN LEAST EXPECTED, KEEPS LIFE **EXCITING** AND, YOUR HOUND HOPES, KEEPS YOU **GUESSING**. OK, SO IT CAN BE A BIT "NOW YOU SEE ME, NOW YOU DON'T" AS IT DASHES ABOUT IN PURSUIT OF **KNOWLEDGE** AND EXCITEMENT. (NEVERTHELESS, PART OF YOUR POOCH ALWAYS KNOWS WHAT'S GOING ON AT HOME BASE.) BUT IT KEEPS YOU PET FOREVER YOUNG IN SPIRIT, AND YOU'LL ALWAYS HAVE AN EAGER, WILLING STAR PAL TO SHARE ADVENTURES WITH.

**T**he Gemini dog is ruled by Mercury, god of intelligence, communication and daily life. When called, this star hound usually responds with alacrity, sensing interesting escapades in the air. In fact, you'd better make sure to come up with something engaging each time your four-footed friend answers your call, even if it's just to tell them (and I mean with spoken words!) how glad you are to see them. Otherwise they just might latch onto someone more interesting and appreciative.

Reading this text on your Gemini canine's complex nature is an excellent step. Being further informed on your pet's makeup will make for better **communication**—extremely important in this star tribe's behavioral lexicon—and lead to more fun, adventure and shared good times.

It's vital, dear owner, that you understand your Gemini dog really does love you. It's just that many of them are not really into great long hugs or lavish bootlicking. (In their book, they "leave that to the Cancer and Pisces animals.") Their agenda is much more about simply being with you, tuned in, and sharing some stimulating activity. As an example: Most Gemini dogs simply **adore** sitting beside their owner in the passenger seat, preferably with the window down, as you zip along in the car. They love to zoom through the world with a fast-moving vista of what they deem "those lesser beings out there." Occasionally, or perhaps not

so occasionally, your star pooch will lean out of the window and tell one of these what it thinks of them.

Your dog needs fast action. It can't stand to be cooped up in one unmoving spot (being chained at the kennel is purgatory). It also likes you to talk to it. Sometimes it will talk back! Not always just vocally. Its face is highly expressive, and its eyes will often be employed to communicate meaning to you. The one thing your Gemini dog would like you to comprehend is that underneath all their sometimes confusing behavior, your star hound is devoted to you.

This pooch can be rather inquisitive, and it can seem to you that it pokes its nose into **everything**. (Forgive your pet if it annoys you sometimes, particularly during its puppy days; it's just that it has a quicksilver nature and it can't resist the quest for knowledge.)

And usually **nothing** is sacred from its investigations. When you have visitors, especially new people or animals, your pooch really likes to give them a good once-over. Perhaps you've had to speak sharply to it on these matters more than once. But the truth is it simply has to know everything that's going on. The Gemini dog likes to gather information. (For this reason many simply **hate** to be leashed.) Some people may call this "nosy," but your dog understands that they are just not hip to its Geminian abilities. If your star pooch could publish a dog newspaper, it would.

Super-alert is what Gemini hounds are. Any movement around your Gemini dog, and quick as a flash it's been noted. Nothing gets past it. But this quality also gives the Gemini canine a rather highly strung nervous system. It can't stand to be teased, annoyed or crazed into a frenzy by kids or adults, who, in your dog's perception, "Should know a whole lot better than to do a dumb thing like torment a dog." (If they absolutely **must**, your dog recommends they pick on a Taurus animal.) If this kind of situation gets out of hand, your dog tends to snap. Such treatment can leave its nerves uncomfortably buzzing. If this happens to Gemini pooches consistently, they can become deeply bitter and untrusting, or react with a nerve-based health disorder. Naturally, your pooch **knows** that you would **never** allow it to get into that kind of state.

Most times the Gemini hound is a light sleeper, sort of with one eye open to keep tabs on "it all." Its attention span is not the world's greatest, and that's mainly because if something doesn't interest Geminis, they get bored super-quick. But never forget, these dogs are particularly intelligent and their mental processes work fast. (Sometimes they're even a step ahead of **you**!) The ongoing activity of daily life interests them greatly, to the extent that on the odd, or perhaps more regular, occasion they've been found watching television or listening to the radio.

Your Gemini dog is good at learning tricks (if it wants to) and your commands. It also has a few tricks of its own up its sleeves. For example, they're very good at making off with unattended—or even attended—bones. Your star creature is also good at demonstrating to you how hurt and wounded it is that you're intending to go somewhere in the car without **them**! Its dramatic abilities are quite good, actually. Even other dogs find this pooch entertaining, **if** your hound decides to turn it on.

Without a shadow of a doubt, this is an outgoing, adventurous, freedom-loving creature. It can also be very winsome and charming if it's after some attention. If its liberty is curbed (its worst nightmare is having to stay alone in some sort of concrete dog box), then its basically joyful spirit suffers immensely. Your Gemini hound has a great need to be able to get out and about, sniff and circulate. Movement is this dog's spice of life. Watch that tail stir up a storm of happiness as you pet finds something particularly interesting to investigate. And watch its tail **go** when it catches sight of you! To this star dog you, esteemed owner, are the most wonderful and interesting creature in the whole world. It thinks that without you, life would be awfully dull and it'd be utterly miserable.

**TO SUM UP:** On your pet's behalf, and without any false modesty, it can be said you have an interesting animal and worthy companion. That tendency to not always do things in the same way, and to come up with something different when least expected, keeps life exciting and, your hound hopes, keeps you guessing. OK, so it can be a bit "now you see me, now you don't" as it dashes about in pursuit of knowledge and excitement. (Nevertheless, part of your pooch always knows what's going on at home base.) But it keeps your pet forever young in spirit, and you'll always have an eager, willing star pal to share adventures with.

The Gemini dog does its rounds of the neighborhood on fleet feet, staying up with what's current. Its quicksilver nature processes information quickly, and this dog is adaptable. If you go about it the right way, your pet can accept most things—even a shift of home base. Despite how it may seem, your dog would like you to understand that it isn't really a wanderer (not like what it calls "those footloose Sagittarians"). The only thing that may cause it to stray is if it gets wind of something extremely interesting going on elsewhere. But this star pooch will never be away long, and will **always** return to you, its beloved and best friend.

This star dog is definitely a charmer. You can also rely on this animal to keep you amused and interested. Your dog's multi-faceted personality will enrich your life. However, do make sure that this canine gets quality sleep, fresh air and peace, otherwise sweetness turns to vinegar. Also make sure to feed your Gemini hound quality food, with high protein and vitamin content to nourish the nervous system.

# CANCER *dog*

22 June–23 July

**tree:** Willow

**metal:** Silver

**day:** Monday

**element:** Water

**deepest dream:** Secret dream is to assist
Florence Nightingale

**celebrity dog:** Fly—the Border Collie who
adopted Babe

I'M SURE YOUR DOG WOULD LIKE TO SPECIFY NOT TO LEAVE IT ABRUPTLY WITHOUT EXPLANATION OR FOR TOO LONG, BECAUSE IT WILL WORRY TERRIBLY AND IS QUITE LIKELY TO BECOME ILL. YOU, DEEPLY BELOVED OWNER, ARE ITS WORLD, AND YOUR CANCER DOG BECOMES TERRIBLY **AGITATED** WHEN ANYTHING SEEMS AMISS WITH YOU. IT WANTS YOU TO JUST TELL IT AND **SHARE** ALL YOUR PROBLEMS WITH IT. YOU'LL FIND THE BEST **LISTENER** YOU'VE EVER HAD. YOUR HOUND'S ELOQUENT EYES AND DEEP **ATTENTION** WILL SHOW THAT. THIS STAR DOG HAS A CERTAIN SAGACITY THAT MAY NOT BE IMMEDIATELY APPARENT. BUT IF YOU REALLY COMMUNICATE WITH YOUR BEST FRIEND, YOU WILL FEEL INSPIRED BY IT. YOUR DOG IS ALWAYS THERE FOR YOU. THE CANCER DOG HAS EVEN BEEN KNOWN TO LIGHTEN LIFE BY ATTEMPTING A FEW COMIC TURNS. IT CAN RANGE FROM FACIAL CONTORTIONS TO A FULL-SCALE TIPPY TOE JIVE!

The Cancer dog's ruling celestial body is the Moon, goddess of the family principle, tides and emotions. This star hound usually turns up right away when you call (unless you've unwittingly hurt its feelings in some way) because it knows you **need** them.

Learning more about the qualities and complexities of your canine's Cancerian nature will benefit both you and your profound hound. As your Cancer dog would see it, this helps you become more understanding of some of its little foibles and more appreciative of its fine, suffering and noble nature. In turn this will increase the quality of your home life together and lead to more love and security as you realize your animal's boundless love for you.

This star pooch profoundly **cares** about its home and family. If anything seems amiss it worries deeply and becomes mournful. It knows these worries aren't always just figments of its imagination because your four-footed companion can pick up on your moods and emotions. Admittedly its own subjective fantasy life is very rich (those dogs who run and twitch in their sleep are more often than not Cancer animals), and it can sometimes confuse these realities (especially in puppy days). But the Cancer canine becomes infinitely better at reading your state of being as it becomes older. And it knows that you **know** this. When you're feeling a bit down, you only have to put your hand on your dog's head to find its eyes gazing at you with all-encompassing understanding. Your pooch likes to be able to make you feel better because of its deep feeling for you.

Luckily, Cancer dogs' owners are rarely down for long—which is good, because the way your hound feels is tied in with how you're doing. You have what is known as an "empathic" relationship. (Well, you might not, but your dog sure does.) When you both cheer up your pooch hopes that, with a bit of luck, you might head off for a walk by the sea together. There it can walk mysteriously and wisely alongside you, now and then bounding off into the waves, or bark inanely at a sea gull. A Cancer canine can be a bit crazy at times.

This star creature enjoys its food immensely. (It's also partial to eating from its very own special bowl!) Eating is **incredibly** important to it, although when upset it can go off its food. Of all dogs a Cancerian animal is the one that looks forward with most anticipation to the next meal. It'll often dream about it. Your star pooch also enjoys a drink of milk. Erratic mealtimes can make it neurotic.

A slobbery dog is usually a Cancer dog. That's because it's filled with the fluids of life (as many a tree and lamppost has found out), not to mention feelings and emotions. A Cancer dog is one that likes to lick, too. Your hound is really sorry if you don't care for the way it can try to plaster licks all over your face at every possible opportunity. This is just its instinctive way of expressing what it feels for you, as is their tendency to bay at the full moon.

Cancer star tribe dogs are also amongst the best at breeding. They make great parents. (They also make great puppies!) This natural nurturing instinct is generally also part of their interaction with children in the family. Your star pooch is extremely protective there, too. Any threat and it's abristle at once, ready to attack and defend unto death. Your hound reacts in the same way to any intruder on what it sees as "our" home territory. Yes, sir! A Cancer dog has strong parenting instincts, so powerful that sometimes it will even "mother" kittens!

One of the things your pooch absolutely loves is to be at your feet in front of a fire—it's all warm, loving and comforting. This is the type of dog that likes to bring in the slippers and then, when you're relaxed, relax itself. Being a rather sensitive animal your pooch isn't really happy unless you are. (It takes most of its cues from you, remember?) If there's the opportunity to snuggle in bed with you in the mornings (or whenever) then that's one of your pet's ideas of heaven. Picnics are another favorite, especially if you remember to pack something special just for them. Your dog likes to busily stake out "our" territory—checking, sometimes a bit fussily, whether it's good enough for "our" family.

Sentimentality, feeling and nostalgia are particularly strong in the Cancer dog—so much so that it may take something of yours (like a sock or an old sweater) and sneak it into its basket. (This pooch likes to have a nice, warm comfortable sleeping space that's all theirs.) There it can keep the smell of you close by and, that way, as your dog sees it, always have a part of you with it.

This star dog can actually love its owner so much that it has a problem with jealousy. It can get moody and resentful towards any competitors (particularly new ones) for your affections. Being a little sly, a Cancer canine is quite capable of giving another creature a nip when you're not looking.

**TO SUM UP:** I'm sure your dog would like to specify not to leave it abruptly without explanation or for too long, because it will worry terribly and is quite likely to become ill. You, deeply beloved owner, are its world, and your Cancer dog becomes terribly agitated when anything seems amiss with you. It wants you to just tell it and share all your problems with it. You'll find the best listener you've ever had. Your hound's eloquent eyes and deep attention will show that. This star dog has a certain sagacity that may not be immediately apparent. But if you really communicate with your best friend, you will feel inspired by it. Your dog is always there for you. The Cancer dog has even been known to lighten life by attempting a few comic turns. It can range from facial contortions to a full-scale tippy toe jive!

But your dog does need to know you love it. Cuddles, hugs, pats, loving tones are all things it can never get enough of. Now it knows that it's even more important to you because you made an effort to find out more about it. (Never forget, your pet's psychic abilities are always picking up!) And your canine would say if it could: "Thank you, my special owner, my heart is yours forever."

### PAWNOTES

The Cancer dog is a very sensitive, caring, feeling animal. Always make sure to let this pooch know of your affection. This way its health, spirit and confidence remain robust, and you'll have a fine companion that's ready to tackle life with you on all levels. A Cancer dog is one that suffers dreadfully when subject to brutality and unkindness. But you, dear owner, will never allow this to happen to your loving pet.

# LEO
*dog*

24 July–23 August

**tree:** Palm

**metal:** Gold

**day:** Sunday

**element:** Fire

**deepest dream:** Secret desire is to belong to the Queen

**celebrity dog:** The Queen Mother's Corgi

**GOURMET FOOD** IS THIS POOCH'S PREFERENCE, AS ARE THE BEST QUALITY DOG-CARE PRODUCTS. BY WAY OF ILLUSTRATION, IF YOUR HOUND COULD SPEAK YOU'D HEAR: "PLEASE DON'T TRY TO TRICK **ME** WITH A **CHEAP** SHAMPOO!" IT'D PROBABLY GO ON TO SAY: "A DIAMOND-STUDDED COLLAR, PLUS A GUCCI LEASH WOULD SUIT ME NICELY." BUT IT'S OK. IT DOES REALIZE YOU PROBABLY CAN'T AFFORD THAT—YET. AND THE FACT IS THAT THIS STAR CREATURE TRULY CONSIDERS THAT THE HOUSEHOLD SHOULD ORBIT AROUND IT. WHEN THAT IS NOT THE CASE, THEN IT WILL USE ALL ITS SCHEMING ADROITNESS TO PULL THE **ATTENTION** THEIR WAY. HOWEVER, AND NOW WE COME TO THE BOTTOM LINE—WHICH IS **YOU**—WITHOUT YOU YOUR STAR HOUND CONSIDERS ITS WORLD LONELY, EMPTY AND MEANINGLESS. TO BE FRANK AND CANDID ON YOUR PET'S BEHALF, IT'S CAPABLE OF LIVING A VERY BASIC LIFESTYLE, JUST SO LONG AS YOU ARE THERE, FREQUENTLY SHOWING IT THAT YOU LOVE IT AND THAT IT'S IMPORTANT TO YOU. BECAUSE YOU **ARE** TO YOUR LEO DOG. IT WOULD DIE FOR YOU IF IT HAD TO.

**T**he Leo dog is ruled by the sun, the creative life force of our solar system and in many cultures worshiped as the god of life and love. This star dog usually has both life and love in abundance. Your pooch nearly always promptly responds when **you** call because it figures there's going to be a good time one way or another.

Reading up on your star hound's leonine nature is just what it would order if able. (Maybe it did! It can move in mysterious ways.) In Leo dog's book you'll then **know** even more clearly what a superior and wonderful animal you are (or should be) the proud owner of. And you'll be even more accepting of the glorious love it bestows upon you, not to mention more accommodating of its "special" needs. You see, Leo canines think they're not really like other dogs. They consider themselves definitely a cut above the rest, so they see the best of everything as naturally their just desserts. And as well as gourmet food and lifestyle (which will be elaborated on later), this star hound considers quality time with **you**, its fiercely loved owner, as definitely its rightful due.

Yes, your hound does know that sometimes you do find its possessive love and need for total attention a little trying. (But it figures that when, dear owner, you own the best in the world, don't you think it deserves the best treatment?) Your Leo canine's fiery, competitive nature is usually quickly aroused when anything else

arises in your shared life orbit that takes your attention away from it. Your pooch is not **always** that open about its tactics here, either. As well as a full-on assertion of rights (your Leo dog's of course), also known as "barking," it's also capable of sly maneuvers. This animal doesn't forget its plans, either, and will wait—sometimes for weeks—for the chance to execute them. But generally whatever your Leo dog does eventually brings a chuckle to your lips. Their cleverness (occasionally deviousness), liveliness and confidence usually end up delighting you, and most times the pooch is forgiven. (But it must be said, whenever **it** is wronged it can take your pet a long time to forgive.) Your smart creature senses that really you love its funny ways.

Wherever and whatever your home together is, your dog deems it "our" castle, and will not tolerate intruders. Mind you, once **you** show it that the human being concerned is permitted to enter, then as your hound gets used to said person, up it'll walk, tail wagging like crazy, eyes bright, ready for homage to be paid to it. This star pooch is definitely not that fond of other animals; except of course for another Leo, once they've decided on which of them is going to rule, and perhaps the odd Aries or Sagittarius creature—particularly when your dog ascertains they've recognized its inherent **superiority**.

One of its most favorite things of all is to recline at your feet as you both gaze into a blazing fire. Other treasured occupations are walking into the sunset or sunrise. Your dog walks regally beside you, head erect, nose up into the breeze, knowing that all who see you are struck by the simple grandeur exhibited as you walk thus together. Of all dogs, the Leo is the one that can be the most dramatic and crafty in drawing attention its way. It can also be quite creative in the ways it pursues attention. Considering itself something of a real star, your hound rather likes a "fan club," and will do all that it can to ensure it gets and keeps one. (This star dog can be particularly good at tricks, both those you teach it and the ones it teaches itself.) Also, when the local dogs need a leader, someone they can look up to, your dog will often fill that role for them. The way your pooch sees it, those "lesser animals" need its golden presence to grace them now and then.

This dog is clever (on the other hand, you might call it "mischievous!"), and adept at getting its own way. But your Leo dog trusts you and loves you peerlessly, so that oftentimes it does bend its will to yours—not always, however. Even though it does consider itself the aristocrat of the dog world, this canine knows how to have fun and enjoyment, and sure adores having good times with you. Having races and rolling about wrestling are just some of the activities that can have you both breathless with laughter and hilarity. But your dog may also enjoy just sitting with you and watching a witty, intelligent television show or video. It likes

theatrical extravaganzas, too. This star dog can mostly be relied on to inspire its owner with its very evident enjoyment of life. (Except of course when something puts its nose out of joint. Your animal is quite capable of hiding away until you find it and put things right. This is not so much because your hound is sensitive but more that it simply can't stand to have its dignity dented.) Without a doubt, life together for you and your star pal is a lot of fun on the whole.

As to lifestyle and how your dog expects to be treated, well it considers it obvious that only the absolute best is good enough. The better the treatment and pampering you give it, the more it'll lap it up and flourish, and so will your royal relationship. Also the more your Leo dog's strong spirit and what it sees as its "brilliant ways" come to the fore, even greater delight and enrichment will be brought to your special bond.

**TO SUM UP:** As mentioned earlier, gourmet food is this pooch's preference, as are the best quality dog-care products. By way of illustration, if your hound could speak you'd hear: "Please don't try to trick **me** with a **cheap** shampoo!" It'd probably go on to say: "A diamond-studded collar, plus a Gucci leash would suit me nicely." But it's OK. It does realize you probably can't afford that—yet. And the fact is that this star creature truly considers that the household should orbit around it. When that is not the case, then it will use all its scheming adroitness to pull the attention their way. However, and now we come to the bottom line—which is **you**—without you your star hound considers its world lonely, empty and meaningless. To be frank and candid on your pet's behalf, it's capable of living a very basic lifestyle, just so long as you are there, frequently showing it that you love it and that it's important to you. Because you **are** to your Leo dog. It would die for you if it had to.

Well, it could sound like the Leo canine's ego towers over Mount Everest and you need a bank vault the same size to fund its lifestyle! But when push comes to shove, the real truth is in the final lines of the last paragraph. The only totally essential item in your dog's world is you, its loving, and beloved owner. However, do be careful not to spoil your charismatic creature, and keep a good balance in the master–dog relationship, otherwise you could find yourself being ruled! Discourage petulance and bossiness. Also don't feed your dog too many rich foods, as the heart can become a vulnerable area for Leo hounds. Bear these cautions in mind and you will have a happy, loyal, splendid animal that will definitely enrich your life.

# VIRGO *dog*

24 August–23 September

**tree:** Hazel

**metal:** Nickel

**day:** Wednesday

**element:** Earth

**deepest dream:** Private ambition is to fetch Rupert Murdoch's newspaper

**celebrity dog:** Snoopy—Charlie Brown's dog

VIRGO DOGS LOVE NEWSPAPERS. (NATURALLY THERE ARE THE ODD ROGUE VIRGO ANIMALS WHO CHEW THEM UP.) IT GIVES YOUR POOCH GREAT **PLEASURE** TO SEE YOU READING YOURS. IT ALSO LIKES TO DO ERRANDS WITH YOU AS YOU TEND TO DAILY NEEDS—THIS ALLOWS IT TO DO A QUICK CHECK-UP ON THINGS IN THE **PROCESS**. BUT YOUR PET WOULD HAVE YOU PLEASE UNDERSTAND THAT IT'S A **SELECTIVE** CREATURE, AND ONE DOESN'T FIND IT ASSOCIATING WITH JUST **ANY** OLD ANIMALS OR PEOPLE. IF SOMEONE OR SOMETHING OFFENDS ITS SENSE OF HOW THINGS SHOULD BE, THEN THERE'S NOT USUALLY A SECOND CHANCE GIVEN. IN ALL THINGS, QUALITY IS FAR MORE IMPORTANT TO THE VIRGO DOG THAN QUANTITY. TO HAVE JUST ITS MUCH-WORSHIPED OWNER AND THE FAMILY IN ITS LIFE CAN BE QUITE ENOUGH FOR THIS STAR POOCH. A QUIET EXISTENCE IS ITS PREFERENCE OVER A RAMBUNCTIOUS ONE, THOUGH IT CAN GET PRETTY ROWDY WHEN PLAYING FETCH. AND THIS DOG'S HEART IS QUITE A SOFT ONE. VIRGO CANINES ARE OFTEN KNOWN TO LOOK AFTER THE HELPLESS. A SEEING-EYE DOG IS MOST OFTEN A FULFILLED VIRGO DOG.

**T**he Virgo dog is ruled by Mercury, god of intelligence, communication and daily movement. The Air side of Mercury rules Gemini, where these aspects are strongest. But Mercury's Earth side adds the qualities of service, application to detail, and healing to the Virgoan hound's make-up. When this star pooch hears its owner call it usually comes at once because its interest is aroused, plus it is another chance to show **you** its devotion.

Your star pal would be gratified by the fact that you care enough to read up on its astro-profile. It's probably looking at you right now, musing on how the quality of your already very good relationship can only improve, and how you will see more clearly the special qualities that make it an excellent pet.

Many Virgoan canines are not terribly demonstrative. For example, they may not jump up and lick with great ebullience at every opportunity. They tend to show their deep love and fidelity in other ways. And some of these are carrying out your commands to the letter, fetching slippers, papers and so on, and watching you closely in an attempt to perceive your next wish. Your Virgoan dog's greatest desire is to serve and please you. If your star hound feels that it isn't useful to you, then it can become quite dejected. To bustle about carrying out your will is your pet's mission in life.

This star dog is a hard worker and will do everything you require. Let's say, for example, that you are a security guard. To be with you on your rounds would be this hound's idea of heaven—not like, your pet would like to point out, those Gemini dogs, that, in your pooch's reckoning, just like to travel in fast vehicles, or those Aries animals that go after **any** action. Your dog's ambition is to be the epitome of efficiency, helping you to do a good job. The Virgo pooch's perceptive abilities are quite strong. It can often tell if something is amiss. The very responsible streak in it would then make sure that it communicated this to you. These star hounds make especially good farm dogs, too.

However, for those Virgo canines not involved in their owner's work situation (which many of them are, as they excel in the working master–dog relationship) they still have a strong drive to be integrated into their owners' lives in a useful way. This star pooch makes a great companion, as satisfying its owner's every wish brings it great happiness.

Accompanying you on visits is something your dog likes to do. Even if it isn't allowed to enter the house and be part of the general discussion, it'll be just as happy to stay outside and gossip with the other animals. Your star hound has an active curious streak and

does like to investigate things. Going for a nice long neighborhood walk with you is another of its favorite activities. Its nose tells it what other households' dogs have been up to, and it quickly notices any change around a residence.

Virgo dogs are reasonably high-strung, not usually in a way that's going to give their beloved owners problems (unless they get treated extraordinarily badly), but more that they're alert to any strange sound or movement. Your pooch would like you to know that its responses are lightning fast. Not that it wishes to sound boastful; heaven forbid! This star dog is actually a modest creature. But getting back to the topic of Virgo pooches' acute perceptions, if this dog is kept too long in an unpredictable or noisy environment, health can suffer. Certainly their spirits sag and their performance falls off. Virgo dogs will worry, fret, and go off their food if subject to bad conditions for too long.

Being neat dogs, Virgos groom themselves well and can be fastidiously tidy. Bones are usually cleanly buried away. Neither do these pooches go about pulling things out (like clothes out of drawers) or chewing things up. (Well, OK, they'll own up—perhaps in puppy days they might have done their share of that.) These canines also adapt well to routine—mealtimes at a usual hour, their **owner**'s daily activities and so forth are what they pace themselves by. If their daily lives become disordered or erratic, this can disrupt their well-being and sense of efficiency. However, if you take the time and trouble to explain any changes in routine to your Virgo hound, it will enable it to cope better.

Your four-footed friend can be highly responsible in carrying out any duties you assign to it. Perfection is something this star dog aims for. But it can be extremely critical of itself if it falls short of its ideals, or **worse**—yours! Your displeasure or criticism can cause it a lot of anguish. But your Virgo pooch can take it, if it's made clear just where it had been going wrong, and what to do to change any cause of disharmony. This dog does learn quite quickly, and as it is **dedicated** to you, your pet is always eager to learn how to increase your happiness.

**TO SUM UP:** Virgo dogs love newspapers. (Naturally there are the odd rogue Virgo animals who chew them up.) It gives your pooch great pleasure to see you reading yours. It also likes to do errands with you as you tend to daily needs—this allows it to do a quick check-up on things in the process. But your pet would have you please understand that it's a selective creature, and one doesn't find it associating with just **any** old animals or people. If someone or something offends its sense of how things should be, then there's not usually a second chance given. In all things, quality is far more important to the Virgo dog than quantity. To have just its much-

worshiped owner and the family in its life can be quite enough for this star pooch. A quiet existence is its preference over a rambunctious one, though it can get pretty rowdy when playing fetch. And this dog's heart is quite a soft one. Virgo canines are often known to look after the helpless. A seeing-eye dog is most often a fulfilled Virgo dog.

There you have it, beloved owner; you now know the deeper strata of your dog's Virgoan nature. You're aware that your pet's love for you is bottomless and that you, dear owner, take priority above everything else in its life. Your Virgo dog's greatest motivating force is to please you.

You have an intelligent and perceptive pet in your Virgo dog. Perhaps it's not as showy as other dogs, but it's definitely capable of extraordinary devotion. This is the type of canine, provided you leave enough of everything to satisfy its needs and the routine is known, that can be trusted inside while you're away. This pooch can be a little fussy over its food and it's best to find out what it thrives on, as its digestive system is finely honed. Do give your star dog lots of love and adequate recognition, as this wonderful companion's greatest joy is to see you and be by your side.

# LIBRA
## *dog*

24 September–23 October

**tree:** Apple

**metal:** Copper

**day:** Friday

**element:** Air

**deepest dream:** To have a celebrity owner, preferably with a Rolls Royce

**celebrity dog:** Lady—from Lady and the Tramp

**COMFORT** IS EXTREMELY IMPORTANT TO YOUR STAR PET. IT WAKES UP SLOWLY AND LUXURIOUSLY FROM A LONG SLEEP, STRETCHING GLORIOUSLY BACK INTO LIFE. THE WARMTH OF THE SUN IS SOMETHING IT LIKES TO INVITE INTO ITS BONES. IT'S ALSO KNOWN FOR OFTEN WANTONLY ROLLING AROUND IN THE SUNLIGHT. FOR THESE REASONS IT MUST BE CONFESSED THAT THE LIBRAN CANINE IS NOT THE WORLD'S GREATEST WORKING DOG. HOWEVER, IT WILL WORK IF NECESSARY, BUT IT WILL TAKE TIME OFF WHENEVER POSSIBLE. THIS DOESN'T MEAN THE LIBRAN DOG ISN'T ROBUST AND DOESN'T ENJOY ACTIVITY— BECAUSE IT IS AND DOES. IN FACT, IT CAN BE, NOW AND THEN, JUST A BIT **FOOLHARDY** IN ITS ACTIVITIES (PROBABLY AIMING FOR EVERYONE'S ATTENTION, IF THE TRUTH BE TOLD). PICTURE THIS EXAMPLE: YOU'VE ALL GONE FOR A PICNIC OR A SUMMER OUTING, AND WHO COMES FLYING OUT FROM OVER THE TOP OF THE WATERFALL WHEN EVERYONE'S SWIMMING? YES, YOUR LIBRAN HOUND. BUT YOUR STAR POOCH **KNOWS** THAT REALLY YOU'RE TREMENDOUSLY **PROUD** OF IT AND LOVE IT FOR ITS INSOUCIANT WAYS.

The Libran dog is ruled by Venus, goddess of love, pleasure and beauty. When you call your star hound's name, it's not usually too long in arriving because it enjoys the interaction, and figures that together you're going to be doing something pretty fun.

Your Libran companion considers it particularly nice that you are making an effort to find out more about it. (Take a look; it **knows** you're having a peek into its complex and cultured make-up.) By doing this you let it know that at least some of its great love is returned. (Yes, believe it or not, on the odd occasion the Libran hound does doubt its central importance.) Your deepening understanding of it will also enable you to enjoy life together even more in your **special** master–dog relationship. The **best** is what your star pooch wants between you.

As you are probably well aware, relationships are of **primary** importance to this Venus-ruled canine. Its bond with you is paramount in its universe, although sometimes you may doubt that. That doubt creeps in because its behavior can seem so full of contradictions. What a very paradoxical pooch this can be. For instance, one time you call it and it'll come bounding up right away, happy and eager to cooperate immediately with what's going on so that everyone can have a good time. Then the next time it'll kind of coolly saunter up and take awhile to be coaxed into active interest.

Another example is the Libran hound's tendency to roar out like Attila the Hun's dog at the sound of some foreign activity outside, frightening the life out of whoever or whatever it is, only to slink under the sofa the next time something similar occurs. The Balances, or Scales if you prefer, associated with its sign can help explain this behavior. You see, the Libran dog is so involved with weighing things up **all** the time that sometimes you catch it on the down dip and other times on the upward swing. Sometimes it manages to get the balance right, but most times this attractive creature is a happy animal anyway.

This is a sophisticated breed of star dog, one with a lot of style. This normally applies across the board, regardless of breed. Even if your pooch doesn't have a pedigree an arm long, it can give the illusion of superior breeding. Even a downright mongrel Libran woofer can still draw the aura of "class" around it when it wishes to. No matter what breed or non-breed they are, these dogs are usually attractive, strong canines.

Being seen with you, its special owner, is something your star hound loves. Strolling along beside you—and in your dog's estimation, both of you looking **wonderful**—as you shop or just get some air, and turning quite a few heads, creates the champagne of your dog's lifestyle. Running along the beach together is another variant on that. We're not talking about an Aries dog–master push-it-to-the-max effort (definitely **not** that!) but a relaxed, more form-and-beauty-in-motion kind of style. Mind you, depending upon the life circumstances, your Libran hound can be just as fulfilled being at your side, listening to the radio or music with you. You are the most **important** aspect of its life if the truth be known. Your dog would like you to know that without you, its heart is empty.

Librans can be the sort of canines that luxuriate in a dog bubble bath. And they're also the type of dog that could easily accept silk and cushions as part of their sleeping arrangements. (They can go with basic if they **must**.) Naturally the best-quality dog products are their choice. (They have no difficulty making their minds up on **that** score!) The more designer labels, the better. This star dog isn't too finicky about food. Of course, it has to be **good** food. Biscuits are generally a favored item. And you'd better watch your pet if there are any chocolate ones around, as it's adept at stealthily filching them from the plate. The Libran dog has quite a sweet tooth.

If you get behind any causes, your dog will be right there, too. It'll march with you, help you with any collections, support you at football—even wear the jersey! Whatever. If it seems right to you, it seems right to your Libran hound. At the end of the day its most important, dedicated cause is **you** and the household. Nevertheless, it can perhaps seem to you at times that this is not so. As this star

creature is a likeable and popular dog, it may have excellent relationships with a number of your friends, which could make you think it's not as devoted as it actually is. So your pooch would like you to please understand that it can relate easily and well to those whom it likes and indeed will set about to charm those people into liking them. But none of these friendships come close to your dog's love for you. In fact, everything else grows out of what your Libran dog feels for you.

**TO SUM UP:** As you may have gathered from previous paragraphs (as if you didn't already know), comfort is extremely important to your star pet. It wakes up slowly and luxuriously from a long sleep, stretching gloriously back into life. The warmth of the sun is something it likes to invite into its bones. It's also known for often wantonly rolling around in the sunlight. For these reasons it must be confessed that the Libran canine is not the world's greatest working dog. However, it will work if necessary, but it will take time off whenever possible. This doesn't mean the Libran dog isn't robust and doesn't enjoy activity—because it is and does. In fact, it can be, now and then, a bit foolhardy in its activities (probably aiming for everyone's attention, if the truth be told). Picture this example: you've all gone for a picnic or a summer outing, and who comes flying out from over the top of the waterfall when everyone's swimming? Yes, your Libran hound. But your star pooch **knows** that really you're tremendously proud of it and love it for its insouciant ways.

I'm sure your charismatic creature would like me to express its heartfelt thanks to its wonderful, fabulous—yes, this is how it perceives you—and beloved owner for wanting to know more about its Libran personality. (They love you for it.) Now you can see that you really do have a good thing going together. The bottom line is that this Libran creature is your loving dog, and is full of pride in its distinguished owner.

Don't take it too literally where "champagne" is mentioned in regard to your dog's lifestyle. On the contrary, you must make certain that all liquids for consumption are clean and of good quality, as the kidneys can become a trouble zone in the Libra dog. Also don't let your pet's behavior confuse you, and never doubt your animal's love for you. You can be sure that any cool behavior that you may encounter is simply a ploy to obtain more attention from you. But give your Libran dog ample love and affection and you have one of the winners of the canine kingdom.

# SCORPIO *dog*

24 October–22 November

**tree:** Chestnut

**metal:** Steel

**day:** Tuesday

**element:** Water

**deepest dream:** To be a member of the dog illuminati

**celebrity dog:** Cerberus—who guards the gates of Hades

YOUR DOG LOVES TO BE WITH YOU, ESPECIALLY WHEN YOU GO OFF ON **ADVENTURES**. FOR INSTANCE, SCORPIOS ARE GOOD SHOOTING AND HUNTING DOGS. NOISE DOESN'T FRIGHTEN THEM, NEITHER DO HARSH CONDITIONS. AND THE SCORPIO CANINE IS **STRONG**. IT LIKES TO STRIKE OUT IN COLD WATER TO RETRIEVE WHATEVER'S BEEN BAGGED. GOING OFF INTO THE WOODS FOR DAYS OR UP INTO THE MOUNTAINS WITH YOU ARE THE SORTS OF ACTIVITIES YOUR HOUND THRIVES ON. THE THRILL OF ADVENTURE YOU DERIVE TOGETHER IS THE NECTAR OF LIFE TO YOUR STAR PET. YOU DON'T HAVE TO TALK TO YOUR SCORPIO DOG A LOT OR DEMONSTRABLY LOVE THEM. JUST BEING WITH YOU IS ENOUGH TO KEEP IT HAPPY. IT'S HARDY, AND WILL EAT JUST ABOUT ANYTHING. (HAVING SAID THAT, THERE CAN BE THE ODD CODDLED SCORPIO CREATURE THAT ACTS A BIT FOOD **FINICKY** AND LOVE NEEDY. THIS BEHAVIOR ARISES FROM NOT TUNING INTO ITS POWER PROPERLY, AND DOG OBEDIENCE SCHOOL WOULD SOON SORT EVERYTHING OUT.) THIS IS A DOG THAT UNDERSTANDS THE POWER OF LOVE, AND IT GIVES IT ALL TO YOU.

**T**he Scorpio dog is ruled by Pluto, god of death, rebirth, sex, magic and atomic weaponry. This star dog usually comes at once when called, as it divines that something of intense interest is about to happen.

Your star hound would be pleased at this opportunity for you to share in some of the deeper secrets of its nature. You may be surprised by what a power-packed, loyal, love-filled animal you have. Your four-footed friend is more than a little complex, and in its estimation, even if just some of this is to be unveiled, it could only bring more energy to the relationship you have as dog and master. I know your prescient pet would like to thank you for your interest in its astrological character, and the love that has motivated this. It proves to your star dog that its love for you, which is the strongest, deepest motivating force in its life—your Scorpio canine would go through Hell to be with you—is the truth.

Scorpio canines have powerful natures and equally powerful desires. They have a certain charismatic force, which they can use to make things go their way. With what your dog deems "lesser canines," they don't have to do anything. These creatures just sense your Scorpio hound's approach, and scamper away in terror. Actually, this probably happens often. Unlike the Aries dog, this Plutonian pooch doesn't have to fight physically. Most of its battles are won on the psychic plane. Part and parcel of this is its secrecy.

This star dog's eyes are usually hooded, and it can be very hard for anyone (even you) to know what it's thinking if it doesn't wish them to. This hound can also have a brooding look in the eyes. When this is the case, it's normally hatching up plots. The Plutonian pup's eyes are extremely intense. The eyes of some Scorpio dogs can be a little scary to others. This is because of the focused knowledge held in them, and is another reason why they often hood them.

A Scorpio dog is one of the bravest under the sun. Any evil-doer encountering a Scorpio hound meets his or her nemesis. This dog will face death itself unflinchingly in a confrontation or carrying out its duties. For this reason Scorpios make excellent police dogs. The Scorpio canine will form a strong bond with its handlers, becoming almost psychically responsive to their commands, and will carry out those commands allowing no obstacle to impede its fulfillment. And this same quality is brought into play when the Scorpio dog guards the home.

This dog never forgets a wrong, either to you, another member of the household or themselves. This Pluto-ruled animal will wait for the moment when it can extract the most satisfaction out of redressing a wrong. And we can be sure that whoever or whatever committed that misdeed will **never** do so again. Your formidable companion is a strong believer in the guilty being punished.

It is a very interesting fact that quite often a Scorpio dog is one with an unusual destiny. (For example, it is highly likely that the 7500-year-old mummified dog in the Cairo Museum is a Scorpio creature.) Strange quirks of fate may dog (pun unintended) this canine's path. Or fate might be seen to take an active role in its life. As an example, a truly special person looking for a dog may unknowingly select from the pound the Scorpio that had been doomed for destruction the next day. As all Scorpio dogs would say: "We can be sure that new owner could never have a more loyal and committed animal."

The Scorpio creature is something of a non-conformist, not in the same way as "those Aquarian canine crazies," as it would express it, but more that it follows the dictates of its own will, not others'. (The exception, of course, is yours. **Your** will is law.) Younger members of your family, in particular—your dog would never hurt them, and would kill those who would—can find it difficult to make this hound obey orders, especially if the dog doesn't wish to comply. Say someone arrives home from school to find this Plutonian pup asleep on their bed, for example. The young person tells it off and kicks it out. They come home the following day, and there's that dog again! Also, among other dogs this one goes its own way. There's not much conformity in these critters. There are qualities of leadership, evinced by their strength and toughness (of all dogs, the Scorpio dog is the toughest and can take and give the most), which other dogs respect and look up to.

Your star pooch may be rather possessive of you. (That's because it loves you so deeply—and forever. It's your pet's nature. It can't help the obsessive love it has for you.) Its eyes will follow you around—if it doesn't physically traipse around after you—and its mind will focus on finding out what you're thinking. The most important single item in this world to your Scorpio hound is **you**. And woe betide those who may wish you any harm. They'll have to deal with your hound first. I doubt that anyone would **ever** survive that.

**TO SUM UP:** Your dog loves to be with you, especially when you go off on adventures. For instance, Scorpios are good shooting and hunting dogs. Noise doesn't frighten them, neither do harsh conditions. And the Scorpio canine is strong. It likes to strike out in cold water to retrieve whatever's been caught. Going off into the woods for days or up into the mountains with you are the sorts of activities your hound thrives on. The thrill of adventure you derive together is the nectar of life to your star pet. You don't have to talk to your Scorpio dog a lot or demonstrably love them. Just being with you is enough to keep it happy. It's hardy, and will eat just about anything. (Having said that, there can be the odd coddled Scorpio creature that acts a bit food finicky and love needy. This behavior arises from not tuning into its power properly, and dog obedience school would soon sort everything out.) This is a dog that understands the power of love, and it gives it all to you.

Well, profoundly loved owner, your dog's glad that this has been revealed to you. Now you'll make an even more powerful team.

### PAWNOTES

You have a strong and somewhat amazing animal. But, despite the reference to your dog not needing great demonstrations of love, it is extremely important that you are sure your star hound knows, without any shadow of a doubt, of your continual love. A bitter and twisted Scorpio dog is very bitter and twisted indeed. If it suffers from brutality, it can in turn be brutal. But keep those love fires burning, and one would be very hard-pressed to find a more capable and finer dog than your Scorpio animal.

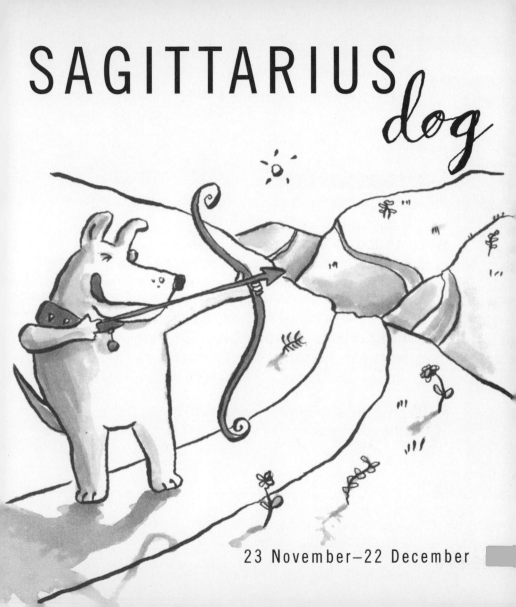

# SAGITTARIUS *dog*

23 November–22 December

**tree:** Oak

**metal:** Tin

**day:** Thursday

**element:** Fire

**deepest dream:** To have been Captain Cook's dog

**celebrity dog:** Duke—the Beverly Hillbillies' dog

DON'T UNDERRATE YOUR PET. IT HAS A VERY STRONG STAKE IN THE HOME AND HOUSEHOLD (WHICH CAN TEND TO INVOLVE PLENTY OF **NOISE**, **TUMBLE** AND **LAUGHTER**). THE SAGITTARIAN POOCH IS ALMOST PATRIOTIC WITH THE STRENGTH OF ITS FEELINGS IN THAT DEPARTMENT. BUT IT'S JUST NOT IN ITS NATURE TO BE THE WORLD'S GREATEST "STAY" DOG. THEREFORE ONE CAN GET THE IDEA THAT HOME AND HEARTH ARE NOT THAT IMPORTANT TO IT. WRONG! WHEN THE CHIPS ARE DOWN THIS STAR CANINE WILL FIGHT TOOTH AND NAIL TO **PROTECT** YOUR DOMAIN. OH, AND ANOTHER THING. IF ANYTHING IS AMISS AT HOME OR SHOULD YOU REALLY NEED YOUR HOUND, IT'LL BE THERE. THE SAGITTARIAN DOG'S INTUITIVE ABILITIES ARE STRONG AND IT'LL TUNE INTO THINGS LIKE THAT.

**T**he Sagittarian dog is ruled by Jupiter, god of good fortune, joviality, travel and good times. (Boy! Does your hound relate to all of those!) When you call your star hound they usually rush right up (alright! it'll slink up if it knows it's in trouble), tail wagging a million miles an hour as it expects you've got an **adventure** in mind.

Your pet is gratified you want to find out more about it. Sneak a look at it if you don't believe me. This pooch is real glad to have more of its canine character revealed, as then you and your four-footed pal will go on to have even more good times. Fun, enjoyment and hilarity are a large part of the Sagittarian woofer's personality (as you probably well know). But this star pooch can be pretty light in the responsibility and commitment departments. It doesn't take too well to stuff that ties it down. If it feels too constrained, then this hound will just bolt. And I know your pet would like it made very clear that it can't abide being tied up for too long or too often; that is sheer hell for its roving spirit (the original "Rover" was a Sagittarian mutt), and it'll bolt for sure at the first opportunity. But your star hound reckons it's a lucky son of a gun and **knows** things won't get that bad for it. Plus it's got **you**! And your pet is convinced that you're so good together that "**Nothing's** gonna change that!"

A good word for this star dog is **optimistic** (we won't mention the word **opportunistic**). Your hound has a great love of life (and of you), and just knows that things will **always** turn out well eventually. Being an enthusiastic and fun-loving animal, the Sagittarian pooch likes to share good vibes with **everyone**! It's puzzled when others aren't that enthusiastic back. "Why shouldn't they like exuberant jumping up, sloppy licks, loud woofing and general roughhousing?" your dog questions. OK, OK. Your dog agrees that sometimes it should tone things down a bit, then adds that it does, doesn't it, when you really make it see your meaning? Anyway, your dog concludes, it's not always **that** rowdy. This pooch can be serious and contemplative as it sits in the sun and gazes into the blue sky, exploring philosophical thoughts and feeling inspirational dreams. Of all dogs this is the one that can seem the most human at times.

But there's also no doubt that this canine star of the Zodiac is a charming and enchanting pooch. It's dazzled many a human being, not to mention other dogs, with its great repertoire of high-spirited and versatile behavior. I shall let your dog take over for the moment: "My rainbow-lit personality has delighted many a soul. It's alright, I've also heard those muttered (wow! wasn't that a clever pun! **mutt**—muttered! get it?) charges leveled at me by meaner

spirits—"flashy, exhibitionistic show-off behavior more likely"—killjoy things like that. I don't care. Gotta do something to liven up life. With my high energy and active imagination, there isn't much that's beyond me." It's as you've just read; reading is believing.

Your Sagittarian dog and you have great times together—swimming, running, wrestling, playing ball, sailing, going out for pizza, church, anything! This hound is an eager and trustworthy companion. When there's action going on you can count on your dog to be in it. ("Action" we said, not "work." Work it's not that hot on.) Your dog even likes to listen to music with you—rock, classical, jazz, country music—they all move this hound dog's rhythm and harmony. Sometimes it'll even try a tune of its own! A colorful life with a colorful master is this dog's recipe for a successful life. And the Sagittarian quality of good judgement is well-known. Like, **you** are its owner, right? It lets you think you did the choosing. That says it all, don't you think?

Nevertheless, this star dog can be a little gullible. This is best explained in its own words: "Some kid might say, 'Here, doggy; come here, doggy. I've got something for you to eat.' Over I'll trot, all expectant, tail wagging, making friendly overtures. Then, you bet, the tyke will snatch their hand away with whatever is in it and run off laughing. I fall for it just about every time. I can be easily side-tracked, too. I'll be wending my way home, intending to get

back to you and dinner before it gets too late; it'll probably be heading that way already. Some other dog then has only to hail me, inviting me into a game I can't miss, and I'm back in the dog house (unfortunate pun—sorry!)" Your pet's expressive eloquence is part of the Sagittarian dynamic, and hard to surpass.

Wandering is something else that goes with this star tribe's territory. That's why Sagittarian pooches love living in the country. There they have miles and miles to explore. There are so many interesting smells and species to speculate upon in those wide open spaces. But Sagittarian dogs can handle the city, no sweat (well, yes, you should leash them as puppies, in case they race impulsively into the street after a butterfly or some such thing) especially when there are parks and/or beaches nearby. Your pet considers those great places for you to ramble over together. But it also figures that you'll always find fun together, no matter what!

**TO SUM UP:** Don't underrate your pet. It has a very strong stake in the home and household (which can tend to involve plenty of noise, tumble and laughter). The Sagittarian pooch is almost patriotic with the strength of its feelings in that department. But it's just not in its nature to be the world's greatest "stay" dog, therefore one can get the idea that home and hearth are not that important to it. Wrong! When the chips are down this star canine will fight tooth and nail to protect your domain. Oh, and another thing. If

anything is amiss at home or should you **really** need your hound, it'll be there. The Sagittarian dog's intuitive abilities are strong and it'll tune into things like that.

So this is your Sagittarian dog. It's a joyous animal, almost invariably in some sort of motion or activity—even if it's just **actively** sleeping—ready to accompany **you**, its terrific owner, into all of life's adventures.

### PAWNOTES

Shyness is definitely not a problem with Sagittarius, as is quite evident from the preceding text. No question about it, you do have a special creature, one endowed with special qualities that inspire, bring laughter, and in general make everybody feel better. People like Sagittarian dogs. However, at heart this animal is your best friend and will always return to your side.

# CAPRICORN *dog*

23 December–20 January

**tree:** Pine

**metal:** Lead

**day:** Saturday

**element:** Earth

**deepest dream:** To belong to the Prime Minister

**celebrity dog:** Nipper—dog in His Master's Voice RCA advertisement

TO YOUR DOG THE HOME, THE FAMILY, YOUR SITUATION TOGETHER, WHATEVER IT IS, IS THE BEST ONE AROUND. AS LONG AS THE CAPRICORN DOG'S OWNER LOVES IT AND WANTS IT THERE, IT CAN GO ANYWHERE, DO ANYTHING. THE MEREST BASICS ARE ENOUGH FOR THIS HOUND. THE OLD DRIFTER'S DOG WAS PROBABLY A CAPRICORN CREATURE. (ON THE OTHER HAND, THERE IS ANOTHER ASPECT TO THE MEMBERS OF THIS ZODIAC STAR TRIBE, WHICH IF PAMPERED AND ALLOWED TO FLOURISH BECOMES VERY STRONG. IT'S CALLED THE "LITTLE DARLING" SYNDROME. THIS STAR CANINE BECOMES SO **CUTE** AND **CLEVER** THAT IT DRAWS ALL SORTS OF LUXURIES AND PETTING ITS WAY— BECOMING EXTRAORDINARILY SNOBBISH IN THE PROCESS! CAPRICORN DOGS ARE ALWAYS SUCCESSFUL, ONE WAY OR ANOTHER. IT JUST MIGHT TAKE THEM A LITTLE MORE TIME.) BUT THESE STAR DOGS DO LOVE A GOOD **BONE**. GNAWING ON A BONE IS ONE OF THEIR GREATEST **PLEASURES**. CRUNCHING INTO GOOD BISCUITS IS SOMETHING ELSE THEY ENJOY. AND PROTECTING THE HOUSEHOLD IS IMPORTANT TO THEM, YOUR DOG WOULD LIKE ME TO POINT OUT. ANY INTRUDERS OR ANY THREATS GET DEALT WITH IN TERMS OF STRICT AND HARSH JUDGEMENT. THERE'S NO MERCY.

**T**he Capricorn dog is ruled by Saturn, god of duty, karma and social structures. This star dog usually responds promptly upon being called, in order to obey your commands and see what's in store.

Your dog would like to say thank you, its "fine and select master," for seeking to find out more about it, as it feels this can only improve the quality of your relationship. The master–dog partnership is **incredibly** important to the Capricorn hound, and it tends to see it in traditional terms ("Not like," your dog whispers to me, "those Sagittarian or Aquarian dogs that consider themselves equal! Harrumph!"). It is the dog, you are the master, and this star dog will carry out your instructions to the letter once you have taught it to respect your authority. Your dog would also like you to know, now that there is this opportunity, that underneath its sometimes cool exterior, it loves you passionately.

The personality of the Capricorn pooch can have a serious cast (but it knows how to be playful, too, which will be elaborated upon later). This hound has a very high sense of responsibility and is dedicated to you. For these reasons Capricorns make good police dogs, as do Scorpio animals. They are not quite as lethal as Scorpio canines because they're a little more cautious and not such risk takers. But an important point to remember is that a Capricorn dog is a long-term winner. This applies not just to the areas of work and duty (out of all the Zodiac members, Capricorns make the very best work dogs—they execute their tasks with great organizational ability), but to life in general. The canine itself would say that this long-term winning quality becomes more obvious when it's put into the equation that **you** are its owner, and its life will be spent with you.

This star dog's loyalty is legendary, and so is its ability to handle crisis situations. (Rin Tin Tin was probably a Capricorn dog.) This is a purposeful and ambitious animal. The Capricorn hound always wants to do better and will plot strategies to attain its goals. That's why it's good if your dog has some involvement with your work situation. It's energy merges right into that, and it will give you all it's got. This star hound has a large appetite for life, so when left to its own devices it will put a lot of time into scheming and then attaining its own plotted ends. Determination is another one of the Capricorn dog's especially strong points.

There can be an air of wisdom about the Capricorn dog. Even as a puppy it is likely to have seemed older in some ways (perhaps there was an ancient, knowing look in its eyes when you caught it regarding you now and then). Fate can play a part in this dog's life, too. For example, it may have come into your ownership in circumstances where strong karmic kismet seemed to be operating. It may have a few minor ailments in puppyhood, but beyond that you are going to have your pet around for quite a while. Capricorn dogs are ones that live for a long time.

Your pet's memory is a good one, and one that reaches right back ("Unlike," it scoffs, "those Gemini canines that exist only in the present!"). Your Capricorn canine remembers things from very long ago that you probably think they've forgotten or things that **you** may have forgotten entirely. In fact, those odd times where you find your pet moody and slightly withdrawn and you don't really understand why, it could well be that they're mulling over something that happened years ago! (That's why it's good to keep them busy and not give them time to brood. Always make your Capricorn hound feel useful, and you've both got it made!) This memory of your dog's is also handy for learning your commands and understanding your ways. Because you are so centrally important to your Capricorn woofer, it dedicates itself to understanding what you want and studying your ways. To that end, your hound's often to be found checking to see what your activities are so that it can add that information to its already comprehensive dossier.

Perhaps somewhat surprisingly, this star hound is not without humor. Precisely because of its serious nature, its comic side is rather droll. Sometimes the expressions the Capricorn dog's face is capable of can crack you up. The Capricorn pooch's playfulness (briefly touched on before) can be a little peculiar, and at times have you wondering, "Is this for real, or is the dog putting me on?" Like for example, your dog finds an old doll, makes it theirs, and then indicates to you it wants to play "fetch the doll." Or it will play hide and seek with you at the most unlikely moments, or perhaps appear draped in some odd garment. In short, the Capricorn dog's playful side can seem slightly bizarre. At times, it's as if it's making fun of you. This is probably correct on both counts. But it adds humor to life, doesn't it? Besides you actually get a real kick out of your dog's antics (which is why it does them anyway), and you see there is a lot more going on in your pet than meets the eye.

**TO SUM UP:** To your dog the home, the family, your situation together, whatever it is, is the best one around. As long as the Capricorn dog's owner loves it and wants it there, it can go anywhere, do anything. The merest basics are enough for this hound. The old drifter's dog was probably a Capricorn creature. (On the other hand, there is another aspect to the members of this Zodiac star tribe, which if pampered and allowed to flourish becomes very strong. It's called the "little darling" syndrome. This star canine becomes so cute and clever that it draws all sorts of luxuries and petting its way—becoming extraordinarily snobbish in the process! As mentioned before, Capricorn dogs are always successful, one way or another. It just might take them a little more time.) But these star dogs do love a good bone. Gnawing on a bone is one of their greatest pleasures. Crunching into good biscuits is something else they enjoy. And protecting the household is important to them, your dog would like me to point out. Therefore any intruders or any threats get dealt with in terms of strict and harsh judgement. There's no mercy. I'll allow your dog to now have its say: "To truly sum up, my beloved owner, all my strong dedication is yours and my love for you eternal."

**PAWNOTES**

The Capricorn canine is definitely a more complex animal than most. There's a wry lovableness about your star dog that you are only allowed to see now and then, as they have strong pride (which can come across as haughtiness) in not seeming too needy. But your dog *does* need to know of your love. Make sure your admirable animal gets this assurance and affection, otherwise feelings of misery and unlovedness can become permanent. What a terrible waste of a treasure of an animal that would be! This one will surprise, amaze and delight you for a long time to come.

# AQUARIUS *dog*

21 January–19 February

**tree:** Moreton Bay Fig

**metal:** Aluminum

**day:** Saturday

**element:** Air

**deepest dream:** To be the next dog in space

**celebrity dog:** Toto—Wizard of Oz dog

BEING A GROUP-MINDED INDIVIDUAL, THIS STAR DOG TENDS TO HAVE A LARGE CIRCLE OF **FRIENDS**, NOT ONLY OTHER DOGS AND OTHER PEOPLE. THIS ANIMAL IS EXTREMELY **LIBERAL-MINDED** AND WILL ASSOCIATE WITH ALL MANNER OF LIVING CREATURES (ONE AQUARIUS DOG I HEARD ABOUT EVEN HAD A FAIRLY MEANINGFUL RELATIONSHIP WITH A GOLDFISH!). AQUARIAN CANINES CAN TAKE A FANCY TO UNLIKELY PEOPLE AND FORM FRIENDSHIPS WITH WIDELY VARYING TYPES OF DOG, FROM WHAT YOU MIGHT CALL A WALKING WORN-OUT OLD CARPET TO THE SNOOTIEST PEDIGREE. (YOUR DOG URGES ME TO ADD: "REMEMBER, WE'VE ALL GOT SOMETHING TO OFFER.") ACTUALLY, OTHER DOGS CAN TEND TO RALLY AROUND YOURS, AND YOUR HOUND WILL RUN WITH THE PACK. BUT ONLY FOR SO LONG, THEN IT NEEDS ITS OWN **SPACE** AGAIN.

**T**he Aquarian dog is ruled by Uranus, god of technology, genius, eccentricity and liberation. When you call your star dog, it's normally right there like flash of lightning. Your pooch is aware that you could be about to launch some great exciting action.

Your dog finds it extremely positive that you have this interest in finding out more about it. I'll let your Aquarian hound tell it like it is: "An astro-profile is a great way to learn more about me (especially as my sign has a strong affinity with astrology). You know, this sort of thing should be done more often. Then everyone would have a better understanding about everyone else, and this world would be a better place. Anyway, back to me specifically. I am glad that I have such an **intelligent** owner. Now let's get on with you finding out more about what makes me tick, so that our life together becomes an even better scene."

Now that the narrative has been handed back to me, I guess it could be said first off that your Aquarian dog is somewhat zany. In puppy days particularly, it may have done what seemed to you like crazy things—like trying to climb trees, hanging upside down, making friends with a possum, eating lettuce—and sometimes your canine's behavior was probably quite beyond your ken! (They might still do all these things and more!) At this juncture your dog wants the narrative back so as to clarify my statements. "Look, this

is not because I've got a 'few screws loose' but because life for me is a continual experiment. (Sometimes my experiments end in failure. Sorry about that.) It's something I must find out about in all its permutations. Those times when you are unable to work out what I'm doing are when I'm operating on my 'genius zones,' so it's OK if you don't understand. But don't stop me. Interference with my freedom of action **will** drive me crazy."

Now that I have the pen back I can relate that this star pooch is a tremendously reasonable animal. It doesn't usually like to make too many demands upon you, apart from the usual food and water plus the odd pat now and then. And Aquarian dogs aren't keen on too many demands being made upon them. Mind you, when you need them to march with you on a picket strike or a freedom rally then they're there for you. Same thing if you want your four-footed pal to watch the outcome of one of your experiments. However, whatever you want your star dog for has to be **interesting**, otherwise it gets bored, yawns and walks away.

Perhaps you're getting the impression that your Aquarian critter doesn't love you—it does, very much. But this hound isn't usually what you'd call 'a sloppy sentimentalist'; it considers that can be left to other dogs. But you are most important to your pet, and it thinks you should know that. The Aquarian dog tends to be extremely intuitive and really quite tuned in to where you're at. (That's why whenever you're really low, you find your pet at your side.) At this point your dog urgently desires the narrative again: "I'm always delighted to see you. Perhaps I don't put on great displays of over-the-top ecstasy, but that doesn't mean I'm not profoundly glad to see you. One look in your eyes tells me more in an instant about how you are than a million bootlickings ever would. Also, when we're doing things together, you catch me taking quick looks at you now and then in order to assess your response. Things always go much better when we're in tune."

As we are seeing, this is an unusual dog. Consequently, it will often belong to an unusual person, and have a home that's different from the norm. Even when that's not ostensibly the case, you can be sure—the dog's grabbed the pen again!—"my unique master, that we have some special purpose in being together. We may not work it out all at once, but there's always a deeper meaning to our shared life on the planet than is immediately apparent.

"By the way, I should point out that there are some Aquarian dogs that don't come across as avant-garde as the way I'm telling this. They can appear more like other dogs and almost qualify as 'normal.' But just dig deep enough, look hard enough and sure enough a streak of strong difference will be found. Each Aquarian dog has an individual personality, even if it's just playing the role of the super-average dog to perfection. Now that is **odd**!"

Phew! Managed to grasp the pen and regain the narrative while your dog was in astounded contemplation of the last sentence. Now let me tell you that the Aquarian dog is a rather "lusty" creature. That is, it enjoys life on all levels. So it usually has a good appetite for food (except for the odd occasion when it becomes so engrossed with what it's doing that it forgets to eat!), plus a great capacity for fun and adventure. Thus, you should be sure to spend a lot of time together where you are just having full-on terrific fun. Your dog's range is pretty comprehensive. If this dog makes up its mind to do so, it can enjoy any kind of activity—sporty, intellectual, artistic, sedate, whatever! If it appeals to both of you, believe me, you can make it work.

**TO SUM UP:** Being a group-minded individual, this star dog tends to have a large circle of friends, not only other dogs and other people. This animal is extremely liberal-minded and will associate with all manner of living creatures (one Aquarius dog I heard about even had a fairly meaningful relationship with a goldfish!). Aquarian canines can take a fancy to unlikely people and form friendships with widely varying types of dog, from what you might call a walking worn-out old carpet to the snootiest pedigree. (Your dog urges me to add: "Remember, we've all got something to offer.") Actually, other dogs can tend to rally around yours, and your hound will run with the pack. But only for so long, then it needs its own space again.

The Aquarian dog's nature is fairly tolerant, and it can put up with a lot. But there comes a certain point when it's had enough, and when that's reached, then that's it! This canine can become exceptionally cranky if not left alone at such times. It also has its fair share of dutifulness and will follow through honorably on whatever its tasks are. In the cause of the household's right to peace and harmony, the Aquarian dog will defend the home with tooth and nail. Despite the fact that you're probably often told: "That dog of yours acts like a human," when it comes down to hearth defense the Aquarian pooch is all dog. It's grabbing the pen again! "And I'm all your dog, my well-loved master."

You have a rather unique animal here (as we have seen in its ability to control the narrative!), one capable not only of adding much enjoyment to your life, but also of somehow bringing a different meaning to things. With this cosmic creature at your side, there are some great moments in store for you. Just make sure that your pet has enough nutritious food and adequate exercise, as it's necessary to keep the blood circulation stimulated in order to maintain health in Aquarian dogs. But with this done, you have a positive, almost electric, top-rating companion.

# PISCES
## *dog*

20 February–20 March

**tree:** Ghost gum

**metal:** Platinum

**day:** Thursday

**element:** Water

**deepest dream:** To meet the Pope on his next visit

**celebrity dog:** Fred Basset—of comic strip fame

THE PISCES DOG TENDS TO BE **SENTIMENTAL** ABOUT ITS HOUSEHOLD, AND HOME IN GENERAL. YOUR DOG EAGERLY WANTS TO HAVE A SAY NOW: "I JUST LOVE EVERYTHING ABOUT IT. AS WELL AS MY FAVORITE PEOPLE, I'VE GOT MY **FAVORITE** ACTIVITIES." [DRAPING ITSELF OVER THE SOFA IS USUALLY ONE OF THEM!—AUTHOR.] "MEALTIME IS ANOTHER FAVORITE, ESPECIALLY IF WE ALL EAT TOGETHER. MY FOOD TASTES A LOT BETTER THEN. IT'S SO MUCH NICER TO ALL DINE AT THE SAME TIME. HOWEVER, THERE'S NO REAL PROBLEM IF IT DOESN'T PAN OUT THAT WAY, AS I'LL JUST WATCH YOU ENJOYING YOUR MEAL, AND MIGHT SCROUNGE THE ODD MORSEL FROM THE TABLE, WHICH, I MIGHT ADD, TASTES LIKE NECTAR, DEFINITE FOOD OF THE GODS! TO ME, NOTHING IS QUITE AS **TASTY** AS WHAT COMES FROM YOUR PLATE. (I LIKE TO SIT AND WATCH TELEVISION WITH YOU, TOO.)"

**T**he Pisces dog is ruled by Neptune, god of images, mysticism and universal love. This star hound likes its name very much because you bestowed it, and upon hearing your call will be there sooner or later, as it happily anticipates some loving and sharing.

Your Piscean animal is so thankful that you **cared** enough about it to want to find out more about its complex, sensitive character. This way you'll gain a deeper understanding of any strange, elusive characteristics it might have, and appreciate how **hard** life can be for it at times. Also, now you'll be better able to enjoy your Pisces pet when its cup runneth over and all it wants to do is **adore** you in its soppy, sloppy, comic way.

The most important thing to understand is that the keynote to this star hound's whole being is **love**. Naturally, as its very special master, you are, in your pet's words, "the most beloved of all owners. I love you **totally**!" It must be said (if it's not already obvious) that your Piscean pooch is utterly dependent on your love. When you're not around it will pine and fret for you. Of course, as a result of its being so, psychically almost, hooked up with you, this star dog is extremely vulnerable. A bad feeling, a harsh word or a thoughtless action can throw it for days. (Too much of this kind of treatment will even make this animal ill.) Your Piscean pooch's love for you is its power source, and, if you'll let it, through its devotion your pet can make you feel better and see more promise in life. The power of the Piscean dog's feeling can have a magic quality about it, provided it's not too bogged down by too much negative emotion. Your pet urgently wants to add something. "The Universe runs on love, and my love for you has an eternal, mystical quality about it."

Pisces dogs generally need a good supply of ongoing, positive encouragement, as their self-esteem can be low, fragile and easily knocked. When their confidence is at a low ebb, their energy gets terribly low, they don't have much interest in anything, and drag themselves lifelessly around or lie wearily brooding and staring into space. Conversely, when these canines' energy levels are high, boy, are they high! They are capable of so much, their confidence is inexhaustible, and they amaze you with their repertoire of exuberant activities. Your star pal positively beams light, love, strength and happiness, and its joy at being with you knows no bounds—so it pays to keep your Pisces pet well-loved. You'll have a much more interesting animal companion then.

It can't be denied that Piscean dogs can have a strong tendency towards escapism. If things get too overwhelming for them then they'll just slip away. These star dogs are actually very good at that. They know all the ploys for disappearing. Also there's not much that can hold them. (One could call this hound the Houdini of dogs!) They will find some way of extricating themselves from any situation—eventually.

Sleeping and dreaming are important mainstays of Piscean dogs' lives, too. They love to lie unfocused in the sun and drift towards "the land of Nod." This activity (yes, for your star creature sleeping/dreaming **is** an activity) helps keep their intuitive abilities honed as well. Your Piscean pet's almost psychic proclivities for reading your state of being stem from that (how often have you felt miserable then been uplifted upon looking down to find your hound's eyes gazing up at you with incredible love and sympathy?). So Piscean pooches need their sleep. For this reason your dog considers it is made for finer things than work. However, because it will do **anything** for you (the Pisces hound is capable of great self-sacrifice), if it **must**, then it will.

If you live near the sea, then as far as your four-footed friend's concerned you reside on the fringe of Heaven. And it likes nothing better than to mosey on down to the seashore with you. Rain or shine, nothing beats that. (It will even tootle on down by itself if you're not available.) Well, rivers, country and parks are pretty good, too, now that your pet comes to consider it. Just so long as you and your pet visit natural beauty, natural places, together now and then (picnics are a great favorite), then all's well in your Piscean dog's world. Your star hound points out: "Like I said before, it's best to keep me happy, not neurotic, because if I get neurotic I can get quite devious and sneaky. (OK, I hear you. Yes, I know I'm pretty good at tiptoeing off with the cat's food.) Sly and cowardly are both terms that can apply to Pisces dogs. But whenever that kind of behavior comes through, you're looking at a dog that has been **dreadfully** and shamefully treated. That's just a way of coping. Poor things. Gosh, I'm just so happy and grateful that **you** own me!"

Being gentle and compassionate, this star dog is usually rather good with kids (unless they are little sadists, of course; that's a different matter). Children enjoy your pooch's company, and it enjoys theirs. As your pet says: "We ramble about together, investigating things. I'll play the games they want, be dressed up by them, be the 'patient' or the 'baby.' Whatever! Just so long as I'm not the 'victim.' "

**TO SUM UP:** The Pisces dog tends to be sentimental about its household, and home in general. Your dog eagerly wants to have a say now: "I just love everything about it. As well as my favorite people, I've got my favorite activities." [Draping itself over the sofa is usually one of them!—Author.] "Mealtime is another favorite, especially if we all eat together. My food tastes a lot better then. It's so much nicer to all dine at the same time. However, there's no real problem if it doesn't pan out that way, as I'll just watch you enjoying your meal, and might scrounge the odd morsel from the table, which, I might add, tastes like nectar, definite food of the gods! To me, nothing is quite as tasty as what comes from your plate. (I like to sit and watch television with you, too.)

"So, glorious owner, let me thank you again for taking this opportunity, as it enables me to give you some insight into the sweep and scope of my emotions. As I keep trying to say, I love you completely. My life is yours. All this wealth of mood and emotion is based on you. Together we make beautiful music."

This is a wonderful, sensitive, and yet strong creature, perhaps not so much in terms of muscle as spirit. Your Piscean animal is extremely attuned to feelings and atmospheres—particularly yours. Make sure your pet feels loved and secure. This doesn't take a lot, just a pat and some daily kind words will do. This reassurance from you will keep your dog's spirits in the positive zone, maintaining its health and happiness. A Pisces dog can be one of the most beautiful animals possible, one that will return your love a thousandfold.

# STAR *dog* OWNERS

(usually called "humans")

# ARIES OWNER

Be prepared for instant action. For example, your owner may seem to be somnambulently reclining around the pool but suddenly leap up, and with a snap of the fingers say: "We're going running, pooch!" Be prepared also for somewhat erratic timing of meals as the latest enthusiasm sweeps all other considerations out of mind for the moment. But the more you welcome the frequent change of pace and new adventures and have no problem being flexible over eating or sleeping arrangements (which could be under the stars, in the back of a ute, or anywhere for that matter!), your owner's love and pride in you will know no bounds. You'll be rewarded with lots of fresh bones and red meat, as well as an exciting lifestyle because your owner won't go anywhere without their best friend, and will make no bones (pun unavoidable) about this. And they will extol the virtues of the best dog around (**you**!) to all and sundry.

**TIP:** Never tire out before your owner does.

**ARIEN OWNERS:** Robert Bruce; King of Scotland; Elle Macpherson; Casanova; Alexander the Great; Diana Ross.

# TAURUS OWNER

If you like nature walks, going camping and having meals at regular times, this could be the owner for you. However, you're going to have to supply unswerving devotion and be prepared to guard the house and generally do as you are told. You might be able to scam along for a little while and think you're getting away with it. Then suddenly you'll hear: "OK, dog! That's **enough**!" as you've just dug up the red rose bush for the umpteenth time. "Heavens," you'll think, "they didn't seem to mind before." That's your mistake. You weren't **observant** enough. Now you're going to have to pull all your best tricks out of the bag or it could be off to the pound with you. So best to start right from puppy days perfecting how to read your sometimes sphinx-like owner and how to be cute and loveable yet also grateful and obedient. The rewards are tremendous. Love, care and wholesome yummy food are lavished upon you, and you are treated as a beloved member of the family.

**TIP:** Don't underestimate your owner.

**TAUREAN OWNERS:** Queen Elizabeth II; Sigmund Freud; Barbra Streisand; Jack Nicholson.

# GEMINI OWNER

Do you like a busy life? Are you able to share your owner's attention? Can you deal with a bit of unpredictability? If you can answer yes to these three you could be on to a good thing. But, and this is the biggest one, are you **intelligent**? You must answer yes to this question to proceed any further. The Gemini owner will expect you to understand given commands and will also anticipate that much instant non-verbal communication will take place through a meeting of minds—yours and your owner's. And this is not confined to four walls. For example, your owner may bump into an old friend, and they'll go for coffee to chat and catch up. Then your owner will be late and you'll have to wait for your dinner. But you are not forgotten. No, sirree! Your owner will beam an information bulletin at you, and expect you to understand exactly what's going on, not to panic, dinner is just delayed. The odd Gemini owner will make it easier by calling and speaking to you via the answering machine. But don't count on it. Work on getting your IQ up from puppy days, impress your owner with the games you think up; always be civilized; and act cool. Your owner will walk you on a Lagerfield leash and drive you around in a convertible as you engage in a very interesting life together. There will never be a dull moment.

**TIP:** Never embarrass your owner by acting uncouth.

**GEMINI OWNERS:** Bob Dylan; Marilyn Monroe; Joan Collins; Errol Flynn; Nicole Kidman.

# CANCER OWNER

If you are able to be **enormously** sympathetic, sit in empathic silences and make caring gestures (bringing a flower inside would do), then this is the owner for you. What you give out will be returned a hundredfold on your owner's up days, and you will always have delicious food. (Cancerian owners are known for their ability to whip up gourmet dog delights.) As a puppy you'll be tended like a baby and have nice soft fluffy blankets in your dog basket. But you **must** be able to cope with your owner's moods. Like the phases of the moon, they're always changing. One day your owner will be limp with despair, and black with the hopelessness of it all. (This is when **you** must stay by their side—no loping off to happier haunts.) The next day you'll have to be up with the dawn and ready to tackle all those great projects lined up. Off you'll go together for a run on the beach or a quick swim in the pool before beginning an energetic and eventful day. Your owner will **never** forget who was there for them in their bleakest hours, and will fiercely love you forever. Your happiness and security are guaranteed.

**TIP:** Learn a few comic routines.

**CANCERIAN OWNERS:** Princess Diana; Julius Caesar; Pamela Anderson; Ernest Hemingway.

# LEO OWNER

"Class" and "best" will be expected of you from this owner. Remember, Leo is the sign associated with royalty, and "regal" will have to be one of your operative words. You don't necessarily need a pedigree a mile long but you do need to have an aura that projects good breeding and noble ancestors. You can be the ugliest mongrel in the world, but if this intangible quality is yours you'll be swept up into protective arms. If you can abide names like "Pharaoh," "Rex" and "Cleopatra" plus fulfill the Leo owner's expectations, this is the owner for you. You'll get lots of coddling, especially as a pup, but also grooming and training. You will be brought out for others to ooh and ah over, much to your owner's delight. And don't be surprised if you spend quite a lot of your time doing the round of the show prize rings. However, it's not **all** shampoo and claw clipping. The Leo owner knows how to have fun, too. You can look forward to sunset walks in the local dog park, lovely vacations in deluxe hotels that specialize in accommodating pets, and total inclusion in all the family's activities. This owner's generous heart, loyal and loving nature (once you've passed the tests—or should we say "finals") will ensure that your every need will be looked after your whole life through.

**TIP:** Never drop your regal bearing in public.
**LEO OWNERS:** Bill Clinton; Princess Anne; Napoleon Bonaparte; Jackie Onassis.

# VIRGO OWNER

As a species, dogs aren't actually known for their cleanliness. But are you able to be a clean and tidy animal inside the house? And are you able to put up with a bit of whimsy? Like for example, would you wear a dog coat made in the clan tartan from the ancient lineage of the Virgoan owner's matriarchal side? Or take heartily to vegetarian dog dinners being served twice a week? That kind of thing. If so, then this could be the owner for whom you are searching. However, are you also **sensitive** and able to see below the surface? Because this is extremely important. You may be an unusually hygienic dog, plus even take to salad with gusto; however, if you can't perceive the deep sensitivity behind the Virgoan owner's organized exterior, then you haven't got a chance. They **expect** that **you**, of all creatures, will recognize the brave soul within, sometimes tortured by the hideousness of this dreadful world, and will share a sacred bond in facing things together. If you can live up to all that's required here, then you will be one very well looked-after dog. A sneeze and you'll be at the vet's. Vitamins will be part of your diet, along with regular walks. And you will hold pride of place in your quietly zany owner's heart.

**TIP:** Make sure to always wipe your feet.

**VIRGOAN OWNERS:** Agatha Christie; Confucius; Greta Garbo; Michael Jackson.

## LIBRA OWNER

Do you feel you have "**star**" quality? Do you think you could mix charmingly with the Libran owner's, sometimes famous, friends? Do you like the high life, but can also be smartly obedient—sometimes anticipating the coming command? In short, are you an attractive and intelligent animal with plenty of chutzpah but able to be at one with your owner's will, able to often spookily follow it before words are spoken? Yes? Then you have found your owner. And don't believe all that nonsense about Libran owners being indecisive. Of course they know their own mind, it's just that sometimes it changes moment by moment—now we're doing this, now we're not, kind of thing. But your being attuned (or you should be!) to your owner's wavelength, you'll have no problem with any constantly evolving scenarios. Don't believe Libran owners are pushovers either. They can be quite strict disciplinarians. So do as you're told and stay off the sofa. Otherwise the rolled up newspaper applied to the rear end will be just what you deserve.

**TIP:** Amuse, adore and obey your owner.

**LIBRAN OWNERS:** Brigitte Bardot; Governor Phillip; Margaret Thatcher; John Lennon.

## SCORPIO OWNER

If you desire an intense and **meaningful** life perhaps you should consider a Scorpio owner. Only, remember, you're going to have to be tough, very tough. You may get tender, loving care in puppy days ("may" mind!), especially if you show promise—that kind of dogged (sorry, pun unintentional) persistence that doesn't give up; the puppy in the litter with an almost supernatural glitter in its eye; the one with an aura of deep magic and mystery. If you can feign this, you'll almost certainly be chosen. But don't forget, you will have to be able to keep it up. When a Scorpio feels cheated, drastic measures are taken. Not only will the pup be returned to whence it came, but the owner will get the place closed down and make sure that full retribution is exacted in every way. See what you're getting yourself into? Still interested? If you are, then you're definitely destined for a Scorpio owner. You'll be silently beside them as you both pad through the night looking for that jerk who ran off with your owner's treasured antique ice bucket ten years ago and is said to be back in town. You'll be beside them, driving into the rainforest or outback or local cemetery for reasons known only to you both. And that's another thing—you are expected to psychically divine your owner's thoughts, as they do yours. Still up to it? Well, you deserve each other. A perfect match. Your owner will **never** allow anything to harm you, and you would fight to the death for them.

**TIP:** Never flinch from anything.

**SCORPIO OWNERS:** Pablo Picasso; Katherine Hepburn; Leonardo di Caprio; Hillary Clinton.

## SAGITTARIUS OWNER

Are you abrim with vim and vitality? Are you a rugged (you can look soft and sweet, but the constitution of a Mallee bull is required) and jolly dog? Do you long for wide open spaces and an owner to explore them with? Don't worry if you have a short attention span and can be a bit rowdy. As with this owner you can count on a lot of variety in life, coupled with plenty of rough and tumble. If this matches your checklist so far, read on. The Sagittarian owner has a big heart and will love you **enormously**. But you will have to have your act together and keep your owner amused and entertained by your unique and wily ways. (It's a good idea to bond with them at once on first meeting to brand yourself on their hearts. Do something cute or clever—clamber onto their lap and refuse to move; stare deeply into their eyes and don't let go of their gaze; then you'll be the pup picked.) If you become boring and unadventurous you might find yourself handed on to someone else. As long as you get your surfing and sage-like skills honed up, you're in for life. This owner can have a reputation for unreliability, but not where you're concerned. There's no food for you because they didn't make it to the store? No problem! They'll just give you the T-bone steak they were going to have.

**TIP:** Cultivate character, and remain interesting.

**SAGITTARIAN OWNERS:** Walt Disney; Margaret Mead; Kerry Packer; Tina Turner.

## CAPRICORN OWNER

If you consider life to be a serious business and can be serious yourself, then you and a Capricorn owner could be the right combination. Remember, a Capricorn owner will usually make their choice for **useful** reasons, like looking for a guard dog for the factory or the house, needing a creature to fetch the paper or otherwise make itself useful, or wanting an animal that's going to add to their prestige in some way. So smarten up and project **efficiency** if you want to attract this owner's attention. But also look as if you know and understand every knock and blow that's dinted that sensitive core, hidden well away behind the business-like surface. The Capricorn owner will feel fate has orchestrated your meeting, and will never let go of the one being that **really** understands that behind their hardworking and, in many cases, unappreciated exterior is a great and noble soul. Actually fate can often forge the link in this animal–owner partnership. If you fulfill your duties **and** maintain your sympathetic bond you will be one well looked-after **and** fulfilled dog. Your owner will make sure you've got plenty of juicy bones after a tiring corporate day as you both wind down listening to the news before seguing into shared sympatico.

**TIP:** Always act purposefully.

**CAPRICORN OWNERS:** Marlene Dietrich; Paul Keating; Sophie, Princess of Wessex; Edgar Allan Poe.

## AQUARIUS OWNER

Are you a bit different or in some way odd, like one eye blue, one brown, or albino or two tails or whatever? But are you also comfortable with your difference and able to project supreme confidence in your unlimited but unique abilities? Then you need look no further than the Aquarian owner. Being at heart unconventional themselves, they will delight in your difference rather than discriminate against you for it, and will instantly recognize a kindred soul in your individual spirit. A bit of ESP would instantly clinch the deal. So try and look wise and knowing. As you head to your new home with your Aquarian owner, prepare to ditch all previous rules and expectations and to play by your owner's original set. These may shift and change according to your owner's relationship with the cosmos, but if your consciousness can keep pace, your well-being will be a fixed constant. You might find yourself eating food from NASA's aborted dog-in-space program, but as with all your basic needs, you will never go hungry. Night walks under the starry firmament looking for UFOs or zooming off in planes to uncharted areas will not be uncommon. And you, being the dog you are, will be in Seventh Heaven as you and your owner enjoy the unusual existence you were destined for. **TIP:** Keep your cool, and don't be surprised by anything.

**AQUARIAN OWNERS:** Germaine Greer; Wolfgang Amadeus Mozart; Oprah Winfrey; Charles Darwin.

## PISCES OWNER

If you're a stray you could have it made here. The word among abandoned dogs is to head for a Pisces-ruled household. Pisceans are known for taking in the lost and forlorn, the ones that **everyone** else has rejected. In most cases they have a soft and tender heart, and know just what it's like to be cruelly treated, and their heart goes out to you. So you could maybe limp a little, or look at them dejectedly but imploringly. However, there is steel in Pisces and sometimes it's well developed. If you hear: "Stupid dog. Think you can con me!" you'd better change tack **immediately**. Straighten your spine, walk right on over, look them in the eye and put your head up for a pat. It will be like mirroring; your new owner will say: "This dog knows how life works," and will snap you up for life at the homestead. Both types of Piscean owners will give you a good life. Although type A might sometimes forget your dinner, preferring you continue watching the soaps together, and type B could also have you sacrifice your dinner because something really important has come up. However, both will make this up to you in spades by giving you special treats. All Pisceans know that in this great sea of life, what goes around, comes around, and want to keep the ledger of love well-balanced with their beloved four-footed friend.

**TIP:** Never chew your owner's shoes.

**PISCEAN OWNERS:** Elizabeth Taylor; Rupert Murdoch; Kiri Te Kanawa; Prince Andrew.

# OTHER BOOKS BY ULYSSES PRESS/SEASTONE

**The Astrological Book of Baby Names**
*Catherine Osbond, $9.95*
A baby-name book with a difference—this charming guide lets you choose a name that directly reflects a newborn's star sign.

**Buddha in Your Backpack: Everyday Buddhism for Teens**
*Franz Metcalf, $12.95*
Explains Buddhism and shows how Buddha's teachings can add a little wisdom to teenagers' high-velocity lives.

**Jesus & Buddha: The Parallel Sayings Illustrated Edition**
*Edited by Marcus Borg       Introduction by Jack Kornfield, $25.00*
Uses exquisite color images to complement the universal truths these two charismatic figures have proclaimed.

**The 7 Healing Chakras: Unlocking Your Body's Energy Centers**
*Brenda Davies, M.D., $14.95*
Explores the essence of chakras, vortices of energy that connect the physical body with the spiritual.

**Starcats: Astrology for Cats**
*Helen Hope, $6.95*
Offers cat owners a unique and charming way to unravel the enigma of their kitty—through their pets' astrological sign.

**The Vastu Home:**
**Harmonize Your Living Space with the Indian Feng Shui**
*Juliet Pegrum, $21.95*
Based on the ancient principles of Vastu Vidya, the Indian art of placement, this book shows how to create a beautiful home interior while bringing a deeper sense of contentment and well-being to life.

**Yoga in Focus: Postures, Sequences and Meditations**
*Jessie Chapman       Photographs by Dhyan, $14.95*
A beautiful celebration of yoga that's both useful for learning the techniques and inspiring in its artistic approach to presenting the body in yoga positions.

**You Don't Have to Sit on the Floor:**
**Making Buddhism Part of Your Everyday Life**
*Jim Pym, $12.95*
Explains Buddha's teachings in easy-to-understand terms and shows how to practice Buddhism while retaining other religious beliefs.

*To order these books call 800-377-2542 or 510-601-8301, fax 510-601-8307, e-mail ulysses@ulyssespress.com, or write to Ulysses Press, P.O. Box 3440, Berkeley, CA 94703. All retail orders are shipped free of charge. California residents must include sales tax. Allow two to three weeks for delivery.*

**Helen Hope**, a well-respected and internationally known astrologer, grew up in a conservative community in New Zealand before going to college in Australia. She studied sociology, anthropology and mathematics at Victoria and Auckland University; however, it was during the three years she lived in Singapore and took time to read the collected works of Carl Jung that she was turned on to astrology. She returned to New Zealand and took intensive, formal training in astrology. Helen now writes regular astrology columns for two magazines—*New Ideas* and *She*. She lives in Australia.